PORCELAIN MARKS
OF THE WORLD

PORCELAIN MARKS OF THE WORLD

EMANUEL POCHE

HAMLYN

London · New York · Sydney · Toronto

Translated by Joy Moss-Kohoutová
Graphic design by Aleš Krejča
© Copyright Artia, Prague 1974
Second impression 1977
Third impression 1978
Designed and produced by Artia for
The Hamlyn Publishing Group Limited
London • New York • Sydney • Toronto
Astronaut House, Feltham, Middlesex, England

ISBN 0 600 39290 2
Printed in Czechoslovakia
by Polygrafia
2/10/01/51-03

PREFACE

This is intended to be a clear and practical handbook that can be used by anyone interested in porcelain. It is devoted entirely to the factory marks on the ware, and is classified on the basis of the actual appearance of such marks, whether these are objects, words or letters. The reproductions of the marks are accompanied by notes on the location of the factory, the owner or company concerned, the period in which the individual mark was used, and the technique employed in marking the items.

Marks used by modellers or decorators are not included. Such information is sometimes useful, but it would swell this book to cumbersome proportions and cut across any aim of making it a work of reference that the general reader can afford. These artists' marks —which, incidentally, have not yet been brought together in a comprehensive publication —can be gleaned from specialist literature based on the kind of marks given here, which are the most important factors in determining when and where porcelain was made. Only in a few instances, where it helps to describe the ware more precisely, have I included an artist's mark.

In general, I have put on record as many porcelain marks as I possibly could, given the size of the book. Many variants which are similar to one another and come from the same factory — such as different ways of writing the same name —had to be omitted (unless they indicated a different date of origin). On the other hand, I have included marks of English bone china, which is not strictly porcelain. For the uninitiated owner of ceramic products, it is often difficult to decide whether a piece is hard-paste or soft-paste porcelain, or even pottery; the shapes, textures and decorative techniques are often quite similar. By learning the provenance of his possessions through this handbook, the collector should be able to solve this and similar problems.

Porcelain Marks of the World is based on my personal experience — on many years of working to build up the porcelain collection of the Prague Museum of Arts and Crafts, which is one of the biggest in Central Europe. On the basis of my own findings, which agree with those of the outstanding ceramicists, I have put together a book which, hopefully, will prove an efficient guide to its subject.

Emanuel Poche

PORCELAIN MARKS
OF THE WORLD

Porcelain marks are not as old as porcelain itself, but they have been used since the early medieval period. Porcelain was made from the 9th century, if not earlier, and the first great centres of production were the Chinese imperial factories in Kiangsi province (11th century); but the oldest surviving porcelain marks date only from the reign of the Ming emperor Hung Wu (1368—98). For centuries the chief marks on Chinese porcelain were imperial reign marks — appropriately enough in view of the world-wide prestige of porcelain and the absolute power of the Chinese emperor. These reign marks, generally known as *nien hao*, consist of six, or in a few cases four, characters. The characters are arranged in two columns which are always read from top to bottom, beginning with the right-hand column. The two upper right-hand characters indicate the dynasty— until 1643 the Ming, then from 1644 to 1912 the Ch'ing or Manchu dynasty. The third character signifies the family name of the ruling emperor, whose other name is given at the top of the left-hand column. The second character in this column means 'period', and the lowest means 'make' or 'made'.

Sometimes the marks are in a horizontal position, with the name of the dynasty missing; in this instance the marks must be read from right to left. The earliest marks were all inscribed by hand in cobalt under the glaze, but from the beginning of the Ch'ing dynasty there also appear imprints made with seals. These are stylized versions of the characters, being squeezed into a square-shape. However, they can be read off in the same order as other marks.

Unlike the marks later used in Europe, Chinese marks are not always reliably dated. The main reason for this was the growing foreign demand for Chinese porcelain, which was particularly noticeable from Ch'ing times. Chinese factories did not hesitate to use the marks of long dead rulers and past years on products intended chiefly for export *(ko huo),* thus endowing them with a spurious antiquity and rarity value. They even used the old forms of the characters. Spotting such frauds therefore requires long experience and great knowledge of the decorative motifs and colours used on porcelain. Only a few specialists have this, and so it is unlikely that most Chinese porcelain which passes as Ming is really original. Many items are 18th- and 19th-century imitations, including some that were even made abroad—in Japan or Europe—and then given Chinese marks.

The same situation exists with regard to Japanese marked porcelain. The Japanese, however, used various special indications that made it clear that older marks were being imitated.

In addition to the imperial marks on Chinese porcelain there are also sometimes date marks. The dates fall within a sixty year system which the Chinese used as a measure of time in the same way as Europeans use centuries. (The sixty year cycle begins with the year 2637 BC!) Since the porcelain marks do not indicate which sixty year cycle is involved, it must be deduced from the characteristics of the object itself. Where they appear at all, there are always two sixty year cycle marks next to each other.

The place name marks can be a further source of confusion. They give no concrete indication of the locality involved, and even the information they do supply is by no means unambiguous. Sometimes they really indicate the place of production, though in unspecific terms; but quite often what they name is the warehouse from which the porcelain was shipped or the merchant who sold it. There are even instances where these marks represent the buyer of the product, his address and similar details. Such inscriptions often had a kind of poetic significance that was perfectly comprehensible to contemporaries, though it is quite meaningless to us.

Equally lacking in significance now are the so-called dedication marks, representing the names of people who are unidentifiable today. More valuable are advertising marks, which recommend the product through a distinctive and exaggerated poetic terminology; this often contains features that enable the expert to date the object. Very useful, but unfortunately very rare, are the signatures of modellers and decorators. Most of their names mean nothing to modern art historians, but they too indicate a year of production which may at least be the true one. Finally, Chinese porcelain has symbolic marks such as the Eight Buddhist symbols, the Eight Precious Things, and the like.

The marks on Chinese porcelain tell us many things. They reveal, indirectly, the structure of the social system of feudal China. They reveal the complexity of Chinese culture and the Chinese spirit. And above all they reveal the great Chinese love of porcelain, and their pride in it as a creation of their own, famous throughout Asia and Europe. In Europe, from the 14th-century report by Marco Polo to the 'discovery' of its components in Saxony at the beginning of the 18th century, porcelain from China and Japan was regarded as something miraculous and very precious, quite on a par with the other treasures of palaces, churches and the mansions of the wealthy.

The marks used by the other major producer of porcelain in eastern Asia—Japan—are of a different nature. As early as the beginning of the 16th century the Japanese discovered that the secret of making porcelain lay in the use of china clay as the main element, a fact that remained unknown to Europeans for another two hundred years. As well as utilizing the knowledge, experience and ingenuity of Chinese porcelain makers, the Japanese adopted the Chinese custom of marking, mostly in Chinese characters, the time and place of origin and even the maker. However, the Japanese marks are more straightforwardly informative than their Chinese counterparts, being laden with none of the allegories and obfuscations dear to the Chinese. In 645 AD the Japanese took over the *nien hao* system of reign marks (called *nengo* in Japanese), but with a different time span. Porcelain products are dated within the framework of these periods, but in view of the fact that until 1873 the Japanese did not use the Gregorian calendar, deciphering these dates is difficult and requires special tables. Furthermore the Japanese too employed the sixty year cycle, but also without properly marking the sequence of the individual periods. (They even imitated the Chinese in dating the cycles back to 2637 BC.) Within each cycle they usually list the individual years, and in view of the scope of this volume it is impossible

9

to discuss these marks in detail. We shall therefore note only those marks that have a concrete content, in other words those that give the place of manufacture (or possibly the maker) and clearly date the product. The Japanese laid much greater stress on such data than the Chinese did. In Japan there was no imperial monopoly, so that there were far more opportunities for business enterprise. Though the marks often carry reminders of 'Great Japan', Japanese porcelain is represented by workshops scattered over almost all the provinces of the empire. The most important were the provinces of Hizen, Kaga and Yamashiro, where the centres of production were the towns of Arita, Kutani and Kyoto, whose porcelain factories created a distinctive style. Their most productive period was the 18th and 19th centuries, when great quantities of porcelain were being exported to Europe. The temptations of the export market often led to the production of pieces that looked older than they really were, and to the imitation of the style in which famous decorators of the past worked.

Japanese porcelain is outstanding for its contrasts of colour. On the one hand there is variety of colours and gilding used to create elaborate painted floral decoration; on the other hand there is the restrained drawing of bamboo shoots and tender leaves. The Japanese strove for a more immediate optical impact than is found in Chinese porcelain, where the aesthetic values are more subtle. The Japanese showed more ingenuity in producing effective decoration, and also made their own technological contribution (cloisonné enamel).

In Europe the marking of porcelain began almost as soon as it was realized that china clay (kaolin) was the main ingredient needed to make true porcelain. This occurred in Saxony at the beginning of the 18th century. However, Europeans had been experimenting for at least a century and a half, and in Italy and France had succeeded in producing versions of soft-paste porcelain. The Medici porcelain of Florence, Saint Cloud ware and other early products were marked, though the object was to record the achievement of the makers rather than to guarantee the authenticity of the objects marked and distinguish them from the wares of competitors.

These motives became important only when Johann Friedrich Böttger, an alchemist in the service of Augustus the Strong, elector of Saxony, discovered how to make hard-paste or true porcelain. The elector hoped to make its manufacture at Meissen, just outside Dresden, a Saxon monopoly, while rulers of neighbouring countries naturally attempted to follow the Saxon example. The first marks used at Meissen were the letters and numbers put on the reverse of each object from 1721; but these were more or less for purposes of registration. Various geometrical marks, incised and painted, were also used, in this case to indicate different types of Oriental porcelain which, for instance, decorated Augustus's Japanese Palace in Dresden.

Böttger's white porcelain was not marked at first; only later did the letters W. R. appear on it. Around 1721 —2 the marking of Meissen porcelain became general practice; the mark used was the so-called Caduceus, which at first resembled Mercury's or Aesculapius' staff. It was used for about ten years, particularly on pieces intended for export. In 1723 another factory mark was introduced, Kite or 'Drachenmarke'.

Apart from these marks, which gave no specific indication of provenance, a mark giving the place of origin was introduced in 1722: the letters M.P.M. (Meissner Porzellanmanufaktur) or K.P.M. (Königliche Porzellanmanufaktur), which were however employed only on pots and sugar basins. A year later a mark was adopted which is used to this day and has become world famous: crossed swords (taken from the coat of arms of Saxony), at first combined with the mark K.P.M. From 1724 the crossed swords mark was used on its own (though it was not officially introduced until 1731), and to this day it is the exclusive mark of Meissen production. At the outset the crossed swords were impressed, but later they were painted in cobalt blue under the glaze, as they have been ever since. Over the centuries the actual drawing of this mark has undergone several alterations. Other marks were also sometimes added, and these often gave their names to the periods in question. Thus during the dot period a dot was placed between the cross-guards of the swords; the term applies to the period 1763—80 although, as Rückert has pointed out, the dot occasionally appeared as early as the 1730's. The same is true of the star between the sword hilts, which gave its name to the star period, when the factory was managed by Count Camillo Marcolini (1774—1814); in this period there were still other additional marks, from which it is possible to deduce the names of the heads of the painting workshop. From the 1760's the quality of inferior items was indicated by incised lines crossing the mark once, twice or

11

three times over or under the swords. Porcelain ordered for the king and his court between 1723 and 1736 carried the monogram AR (Augustus Rex). Special marks were also made on porcelain manufactured for the Saxon court in Dresden and in Warsaw (Augustus being king of Poland as well as elector of Saxony).

Apart from factory marks, some products of the 1730's carried impressed marks made by the modeller; then, in 1740, modellers' marks were replaced by numerals. Finally, the numbering of models, carried out retrospectively in 1749 when the manufacture was directed by J. J. Kändler, added to the difficulty of deciphering Meissen markings. Such was the productivity of Meissen that by 1764 no less than 3051 models had been registered.

The crossed swords mark is the oldest European porcelain mark that is still in use. It symbolizes an output which, in the 18th century, and particularly thanks to J.J. Kändler, achieved the status of high art. As such it had a tremendous influence on contemporary culture, of which it gives us an especially vivid picture.

It is interesting that Meissen's closest competitor, the factory in imperial Vienna, left its products unmarked for nearly three decades. This can hardly be explained by the involvement of private enterprise in the person of Claudius Innocentius du Paquier, since the Berlin entrepreneur Wegely marked his ware with his own monogram. Apparently du Paquier did not mark ware from his factory for the simple reason that it was not yet custom in 1718, when he started production.

Viennese porcelain began to be marked only when the factory was bought by the state in 1744. The mark chosen was the emblem of the duchy of Austria, a heraldic shield with a beam across it. Its shape gave rise to the erroneous belief that it was intended to represent a beehive. The Viennese imperial porcelain factory employed this mark, which was first impressed, then painted, and later still impressed again, for more than a hundred years, until the factory closed in 1864.

As well as the factory mark, Vienna porcelain carried complicated subsidiary markings which provided information about the maker and the date of production. In the 18th century porcelain figures carried modellers' marks in the form of various impressed letters; in the 19th century the presence of painted numerals provided information about several generations of painters of all genres —figure painters and decorative painters, and painters of landscapes and still-lifes. The factory also indicated the year of production with impressed numbers; and the practice was copied by several other porcelain factories in the Austro-Hungarian Empire, including the Czech factories at Slavkov and Klášterec nad Ohří.

With the expansion of porcelain production in the German states and throughout Europe in the later 18th century, marking systems became the rule. Royal and aristocratic entrepreneurs, stimulated by the achievements of the factories at Meissen, Vienna and Venice, vied with one another in setting up their own concerns, and in the process developed a number of systems of marking porcelain. The two Ls monogram of Louis XV appeared on Sèvres porcelain, and in the 18th and 19th centuries the monograms of various monarchs, shown with a crown, were commonly seen. But an even more popular way of marking porcelain in the 19th century was to use a symbolic motif. The symbol of the state or ruler was shown through some heraldic device (a coat of arms, or certain elements of one, or else the ruler's insignia), often followed by a symbol representing the place of production. In addition to the heraldic marks already mentioned, there are those of St Petersburg, Nymphenburg and Herend, and of Italian and Spanish porcelain. In the second category it is possible to include the silhouette of the dome of Florence Cathedral on Medici porcelain, as well as the motif of the sea on Copenhagen porcelain; and there are a good many others.

With the further expansion of porcelain production in the 19th century, the period of the industrial revolution, hundreds and hundreds of new porcelain factories sprang up. The resulting fierce competition, haste and mechanization of production did not encourage painstaking differentiation between marks by means of symbols. It became the practice for a firm to follow the English example and simply give its name, either in full or in abbreviated form, which sufficiently indicated the locality and/or ownership of the company. The symbol, where it was still used, became at best a minor decorative motif. There were fewer hand-written marks, and with the introduction of copperplate printing on porcelain (also based on the English model) printed marks made with a stamp became commonplace. But the desire for profit or the need to survive sometimes came into conflict with the principle of correct marking. In such cases, marks were altered so as to resemble the symbols or monograms of the factories manufacturing the best wares. This tendency had been in evidence from the earliest days of European porcelain; at Meissen, for example, Böttger's products had been inscribed with Oriental, usually Chinese, characters and symbols. Similarly, 18th-century English businessmen at Derby, Worcester and Caughley did not hesitate to use quasi-Oriental marks, tacitly claiming that their ware was comparable in quality to Oriental porcelain. These earlier practices concealed no fraudulent intentions; they were, rather, an expression of admiration and respect for centuries of Oriental tradition, as well as representing an attempt to exploit its popularity. In the 19th century, practices of this sort were less innocent in intention. Many marks were intended to create the impression that the ware had been produced at one of the great European centres. The Meissen mark was imitated in England (at Chelsea, Derby, Worcester and Bristol), in Belgium (at Tournai), in Holland (at Weesp), and in Germany itself at such factories as Rauenstein, Limbach, Nymphenburg, Volkstedt and Wallendorf. In Bohemia the Loket and Dubí factories imitated Meissen; and as far away as Russia the Englishman Francis Gardner did the same at Verbilki. Sèvres porcelain, with its world-wide reputation, also proved a magnet for imitators, who copied the famous intertwined Ls; among the imitators were the factories at Valenciennes, Limoges and Foëcy in France, Derby and Worcester in England, and several lesser known porcelain factories in Germany. The mark of the imperial factory in Vienna was imitated too, but not so blatantly as the Sèvres and Meissen marks—probably because the Viennese factory was gradually declining in importance. But a modern firm that has complicated the identification of Viennese porcelain is the Vienna-Augarten, which since 1922 has been manufacturing ware in modern styles, but has also produced historicizing porcelain, including tableware with subjects taken from the Neo-Classical Sorgenthal period.

The leading factories naturally did their best to protect themselves against imitation of their marks, even if only a general similarity was involved. The effectiveness of such imitations was thus often ephemeral. Yet such forgeries and imitations have managed to deceive experienced collectors and the curators of museum collections, and it has therefore become necessary to devote increased attention to marks and to assess them in the context of the overall character of the object concerned. In trying to discover where and when it was made, the basic criterion is always the nature of the material used. In certain cases this can be an absolutely decisive consideration. For example, some porcelain factories have disposed of — still dispose of — original models from which new casts can be taken again and again. Superficially there may be no way of telling whether an object is two years or two hundred years old. This is most notoriously true of Meissen, but it also applies to Höchst, whose models were taken over by the factory at Damm, which even used the same mark as Höchst. This, however, was merely an episode around 1800, whereas Meissen 'Rococo porcelain' is manufactured to this day with 18th-century lavishness and superb technique. The Berlin factory too has made new casts from 18th-century models. However, since the 19th century Berlin has used different marks for its products, including casts made from 18th-century models; so there is no difficulty in distinguishing between the old and the new.

Where the mark is the same, detailed examination will generally show up the differences. The body of a modern cast is usually smooth and unbroken; for instance the bases of the figures are not cracked. The glaze is brilliant and shiny, and the tones of the colours often differ from those of the 18th-century palette. This is particularly true of the countless idyllic Rococo-like figures and groups which, thanks to their decorative charm, remain enormously popular with the public at large.

Modern copies of tableware are even easier to spot. Copyists make all sorts of mistakes as to both the shape of the ware — overemphasizing its 'period' features — and its painted decoration. Modern decorators are never as successful as their 18th- and early 19th-century predecessors in creating Rococo and Neo-Classical subjects such as flowers, landscapes, figures and scenes. In particular, they find it impossible to simulate the brushwork of the old painters. Even in China and Japan, where imitating ancient models was a traditional occupation (pursued with such success by the 18th century that the results were often indistinguishable from the originals), the craft declined in the 19th century. Here too the copy is always given away by the brushstrokes, the subject matter, or the composition of the materials employed.

It should be clear from all this that the authenticity of marks must always be verified. The mark must be examined with the character of the object itself in mind, and all the more so since porcelain is perhaps the only art in which historicism is still alive today. Deliberate forgeries apart, there is a continuing popular demand for pseudo-Rococo tableware and modern 'kitch' reproductions of the Empire style. Porcelain lends itself perfectly to Rococo and Neo-Classicism, with the result that these have become the accepted styles for any artistic work in the medium. Only modern utility porcelain, and some decorative porcelain produced by outstanding artists at such factories as Sèvres, Copenhagen, Ludwigsburg and Meissen, have broken with tradition and struck any kind of modern note.

And this may change in the future. For although this once precious material has become a daily commonplace, its qualities are such that it is unlikely ever to be replaced by some modern synthetic material.

MARKS

NOTE ON THE CLASSIFICATION
OF MARKS

The marks in this book are grouped according to their subject matter. This seemed the arrangement best suited to the practical needs of readers, for whom the factory mark of an object is the chief and most reliable indication of when, where and by whom it was made. One group here consists of marks whose main motifs are pictorial symbols, in another and much larger group the main features are place names, or the names or monograms of the producers. However, it is a very difficult matter to classify all the marks so unambiguously since some of them are composed of more than one symbol. In such cases the author could only decide for himself to which group a particular mark belonged. For this reason, when readers are investigating a mark they should check up on all the motifs to be found on it.

The sequence of groups is as follows: the sun 1—7; the moon 8—19; the stars 20—30; water 31—3; flora 34—79; man and parts of his body 80—87; fauna 88—122; insignia and heraldic devices 123—234; emblems 235—6; 'Zachenbalken' 237—8; arms 239—55; implements, instruments and machines 256—313; buildings 314—28; symbols and geometric motifs 329—59; Roman alphabet marks 360—1738; Cyrillic alphabet marks 1739—1801; Oriental marks 1802——2031; European imitations of Oriental marks 2032—2061.

LIST OF ABBREVIATIONS

B	Belgium
DK	Denmark
DDR	German Democratic Republic
D	German Federal Republic
GB	Great Britain
F	France
N	Netherlands
IRL	Ireland
I	Italy
J	Japan
YU	Yugoslavia
L	Luxembourg
PL	Poland
P	Portugal
R	Rumania
SU	USSR
S	Sweden
CH	Switzerland
E	Spain
CS	Czechoslovakia
H	Hungary

1		**SAINT CLOUD** Royal Porcelain Factory 1693—1722 / *blue*
2		**SAINT CLOUD** Royal Porcelain Factory 1693—1722 / *blue*
3		**SAINT CLOUD** Royal Porcelain Factory 1693—1722 / *blue*
4		**VOLKSTEDT-RUDOLSTADT** H. Greiner 1808—1870 / *blue*
5		**LICHTE** Heubach Bros 19th cent. / *printed*
6		**TURN** (Trnovany) Riessner & Kessel, "Amphora" from 1892 / *printed*
7		**SCHIRNDING** Porzellanfabrik from 1902 / *printed*
8		**BOW** W. Duesbury 1762—1776 / *blue*
9		**WORCESTER** Dr Wall 1751—1783 / *blue*
10		**WORCESTER** Dr Wall 1751—1783 / *red*

11	**WORCESTER** Dr Wall 1751—1783 / *red*
12	**LOWESTOFT** imitations of Worcester 2nd half of 18th cent. / *blue*
13 **14**	**CAUGHLEY** T. Turner 1772—1799 / *blue*
15 **16**	**CAUGHLEY** T. Turner 1772—1799 / *blue*
17	**PINXTON** W. Billingsley 1796—1813 / *red*
18	**COPENHAGEN** Royal Porcelain Factory 19th cent. / *impressed*
19	**OESLAU** W. Goebel from 1879 / *printed*
20	**DOCCIA** L. Ginori 1770—1790 / *red*
21	**DOCCIA** C. L. Ginori late 18th—early 19th cent. *blue, red, gold*
22 **23** **24**	**DOCCIA** C. L. Ginori late 18th —early 19th cent. / *blue*
25	**DOCCIA** Ginori late 19th cent. / *impressed*
26 **27**	**LE NOVE** E. P. Antonibon from 1763 / *red, gold* / *blue, red, gold*

28		LONGTON Paragon China Ltd. from 1919 / *printed*
29		NOVGOROD Kuznetsov 1st half of 19th cent. / *blue*
30		TOMASZOW M. Mezer 1806—1810 / *printed*
31		COPENHAGEN Royal Porcelain Factory 1830—1845 / *blue*
32		COPENHAGEN Royal Porcelain Factory 1830—1845 / *blue*
33		COPENHAGEN Royal Porcelain Factory 1830—1845 / *blue*
34		SCHLAGGENWALD (Slavkov) Haas & Czjizek 1888—1906 / *printed*
35		SCHLAGGENWALD (Slavkov) Haas & Czjizek 20th cent. / *printed*
36		SCHLAGGENWALD (Slavkov) Haas & Czjizek 1888—1896 / *printed*
37		CHODAU (Chodov) Haas & Czjizek from 1905 / *printed*

38		WALDENBURG (Walbrzych) Krister Porzellanmanufaktur 1831—1943 / *blue*
	C K W	
39		REHAU Zeh, Scherzer & Co. from 1880 / *printed*
	GERMANY	
40		CAPODIMONTE Royal Porcelain Factory 1743—1759 / *impressed*
41		PARIS, PONT AUX CHOUX "Mignon" 1777—1784 / *blue*
42		SAINT CLOUD Royal Porcelain Factory 1696 / *incised*
43 44		PARIS, PONT AUX CHOUX "Mignon" 1777—1784 / *blue*
45 46		CAPODIMONTE Royal Porcelain Factory 1743—1759 / *blue*
47		BUEN RETIRO Royal Porcelain Factory 1760—1803 / *blue*
48		CAPODIMONTE Royal Porcelain Factory 1743—1759 / *blue*
49 50 51		BUEN RETIRO Royal Porcelain Factory 1760—1803 / *blue*
52		BUEN RETIRO Royal Porcelain Factory 1760—1803 / *blue*

53		CHELSEA N. Sprimont & C. Gouyn 1745—1749 / *blue*
54		LIMBACH G. Greiner after 1787 / *red, green, gold, black*
55 56		KLOSTER VEILSDORF G. Greiner 1797—1822 / *blue*
57		ORLÉANS Manufacture Royale after 1753(?) or after 1766 / *blue*
58		PARIS, RUE DE LA ROQUETTE Souroux after 1773 / *blue, red*
59		CHARLOTTENBRUNN (Zofiówka) J. Schachtel after 1859 / *printed*
60		ALT-ROHLAU (Stará Role) M. Zdekauer after 1881 / *printed*
61		NIEDERSALZBRUNN (Szczawienko) H. Ohme after 1882 / *printed*
62		WUNSIEDEL Retsch & Co. after 1885 / *printed*
63		WUNSIEDEL Retsch & Co. after 1885 / *printed*

64		COALPORT J. Rose after 1796 / *printed*
65		MERKELSGRÜN (Merklín) 1881—1918 / *printed*
66		MARKTREDWITZ Jaeger & Co. after 1872 / *printed*
67		SCHAALA H. Voigt after 1872 / *printed*
68		POTSCHAPPEL C. Thieme after 1872 / *printed*
69		LICHTE Heubach Bros after 1820 / *blue*
70		PLAUE C. G. Schierholz & Sohn after 1817 / *blue*
71		PLAUE C. G. Schierholz & Sohn after 1817 / *printed*
72		PLAUE C. G. Schierholz & Sohn after 1817 / *printed*

73		GROSSBREITENBACH G. Greiner after 1783 / *blue*
74		LIMBACH G. Greiner after 1787 / *blue*
75		ILMENAU G. Greiner 1787—1792 / *blue*
76		LIMBACH Porcelain Factory middle of 19th cent. *printed*
77		GROSSBREITENBACH H. Bühl & Söhne 19th cent. / *printed*
78		DUX (Duchcov) E. Eichler after 1860 / *printed*
79		GEHREN J. Günthersfeld & Co. after 1884 / *printed*
80		MILAN San Cristoforo after 1945 / *printed*
81		VIENNA, WILHELMSBURG Oest. Keramik A. G. 1883—1945 / *printed*

82		**OHRDRUF** Baehr & Proeschild after 1871 / *printed*
83		**ELBOGEN** (Loket) R. & F. Haidinger 1815—1833 / *blue*
84		**ELBOGEN** (Loket) R. & F. Haidinger 1833—1860 / *impressed*
85		**ELBOGEN** (Loket) Springer & Co. *c.* 1900 / *blue*
86		**ELBOGEN** (Loket) "Epiag" 1938—1945 / *blue*
87		**PÖSSNECK** Conta & Böhme after 1790 / *blue*
88		**KASSEL** Friedrich II of Hesse-Kassel 1766—1788 / *blue*
89		**FRANKENTHAL** J. A. Hannong 1756—1759 / *blue*
90		**MARKTSCHWABEN** Keramische Fabrik 19th cent. / *printed*

91	**HEREND** Porcelain Factory 1897 / *printed*
92	**TETTAU** G. C. Greiner after 1885 / *gold*
93	**SWINTON** Royal Rockingham Works 1820—1842 / *printed*
94	**FÜRSTENBERG** Fürstliche Porzellanmanufactur 1770—1814 / *impressed*
95	**UNTERWEISSBACH** Mann & Porzelius A. G. 19th cent. / *printed*
96	**KLÖSTERLE** (Klášterec) M. Weber 1796—1803 / *red, black*
97 **98**	**KLÖSTERLE** (Klášterec) M. Weber 1804—1830 / *blue, various colours*
99	**LUDWIGSBURG** Carl Eugen of Württemberg 1759—1806 / *blue*
100	**LUDWIGSBURG** Carl Eugen of Württemberg 1759—1806 / *blue*

101	**LUDWIGSBURG** Carl Eugen of Württemberg 1759—1806 / *blue*
102	**KATZHÜTTE** Hertwig & Co. 19th cent. until 1945 / *impressed*
103 **104**	**HAGUE** A. & J. F. Lynker 1776—1790 / *blue*
105	**HAGUE** A. & J. F. Lynker 1776—1790 / *blue*
106	**HAGUE** A. & J. F. Lynker 1776—1790 / *blue*
107	**SUHL** E. Schlegelmilch after 1861 / *printed*
108	**VIENNA, WILHELMSBURG** Oest. Keramik A. G. 1883—1945 / *printed*
109	**FENTON** E. Brain & Co. after 1900 / *printed*
110	**BARCELONA** Manufacturas Cerámicas after 1921 / *printed*

111	MARKTREDWITZ Jaeger & Co. after 1872 / *printed*
112 	ANSBACH Markgräfliche Porzellan- manufaktur 1758—1790 / *blue*
113	ANSBACH Markgräfliche Porzellan- manufaktur 1758—1790 / *blue*
114 **115** 	NYON J. Dortu & F. Müller 1781—1813 / *blue*
116	KÖPPELSDORF J. Hering & Sohn after 1893 / *printed*
117	LILLE Leperre-Durot 1784—1817 / *red*
118	LILLE Leperre-Durot 1784—1817 / *red*
119 	MITTERTEICH M. Emanuel & Co. after 1900 / *printed*

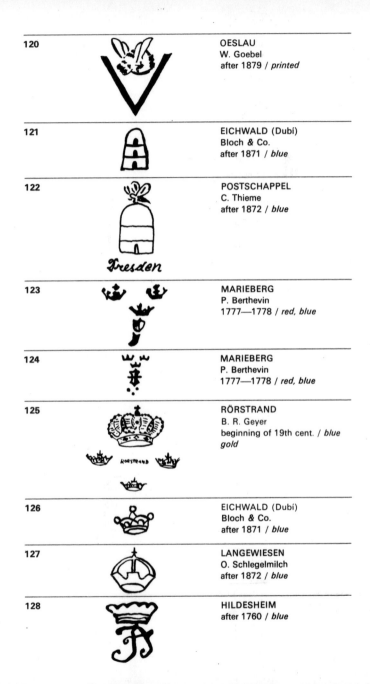

120	**OESLAU** W. Goebel after 1879 / *printed*
121	**EICHWALD (Dubí)** Bloch & Co. after 1871 / *blue*
122	**POSTSCHAPPEL** C. Thieme after 1872 / *blue*
123	**MARIEBERG** P. Berthevin 1777—1778 / *red, blue*
124	**MARIEBERG** P. Berthevin 1777—1778 / *red, blue*
125	**RÖRSTRAND** B. R. Geyer beginning of 19th cent. / *blue* *gold*
126	**EICHWALD (Dubí)** Bloch & Co. after 1871 / *blue*
127	**LANGEWIESEN** O. Schlegelmilch after 1872 / *blue*
128	**HILDESHEIM** after 1760 / *blue*

129		**BUEN RETIRO** Charles III of Spain after 1759 / *blue*
130		**DERBY** Crown Porcelain Co. 1877—1889 / *printed*
131		**DERBY** Crown Porcelain Co. after 1890 / *printed*
132		**DERBY** Crown Porcelain Co. 1784—1811 / *gold*
133		**BOCK-WALLENDORF** Fasold & Stauch after 1903 / *printed*
134		**WORCESTER** Royal Worcester Porcelain Co. from 1862 / *printed*
135		**FENTON** Crown Staffordshire China after 1801 / *printed*
136		**FISCHERN (Rybáře)** C. Knoll beginning of 20th cent. / *printed*

137	**WALDENBURG (Walbrzych)**
	C. Tielsch
	2nd half of 19th cent. / *blue*

138	**PIRKENHAMMER (Březová)**
	after 1890 until 1938 / *red, printed*

139	**COPENHAGEN**
	Royal Porcelain Factory
	1905 / *gold*

140	**COPENHAGEN**
	Royal Porcelain Factory
	1905 / *gold*

141	**COPENHAGEN**
	Royal Porcelain Factory
	from 1929 / *gold*

142	**KAHLA**
	Porcelain Factory
	after 1844 / *printed*

143	**ELLWANGEN**
	A. F. Prahl's widow
	c. 1760 / *blue*

144	**ELLWANGEN**
	A. F. Prahl's widow
	c. 1760 / *blue*

145

HELSINKI
Arabia A/B
1874—1917 / *printed*

146

HEREND
Porcelain Factory
c. 1850 / *blue*

147

HEREND
Porcelain Factory
1900—1934 / *blue*

148

HEREND
Porcelain Factory
1891—1897 / *blue*

149

FRYAZINO
Barmin Bros
1820—1850 / *blue*

150

HOHENBERG
C. M. Hutschenreuther
1865 / *printed*

151

BADEN-BADEN
Z. Pfalzer
1771—1778 / *blue*

152

SAARGEMÜND
Utzschneider & Co.
19th cent. / *printed*

153 	SAARGEMÜND Utzschneider & Co. 19th cent. / *printed*
154	TURN (Trnovany) E. Wahliss, "Alexandra- Porcelain-Works" after 1894 / *printed*
155 **156**	TIRSCHENREUTH Porzellanfabrik 2nd half of 19th cent. / *printed*
157	TURN (Trnovany) E. Wahliss, "Alexandra- Porcelain-Works" after 1894 / *printed*
158	HELSINKI Arabia A/B after 1874 / *printed*
159 **160** 	REHAU Zeh, Scherzer & Co. *c.* 1900 / *printed*
161	ANSBACH Markgräfliche Porzellan- manufaktur last quarter of 18th cent. *impressed*
162	ANSBACH Markgräfliche Porzellan- manufaktur *c.* 1765 and 19th cent. / *blue*

163	**ANSBACH** Markgräfliche Porzellan- manufaktur *c.* 1765 and 19th cent. / *blue*
164	**VIENNA** Staatsmanufaktur 2nd half of 18th cent. / *blue*
165	**VIENNA** Staatsmanufaktur 1744—1749 / *incised*
166	**VIENNA** Staatsmanufaktur 1749—1820 / *blue*
167	**VIENNA** Staatsmanufaktur 1744—1749 / *impressed*
168	**VIENNA** Staatsmanufaktur 1820—1827 / *blue*
169	**VIENNA** Staatsmanufaktur 1760—1770 / *blue*
170 **171**	**NYMPHENBURG** Kurfürstliche Porzellan- manufaktur 1755—1765 / *impressed*
172	**NYMPHENBURG** Kurfürstliche Porzellan- manufaktur 1810—1850 / *impressed*
173	**NYMPHENBURG** Kurfürstliche Porzellan- manufaktur 1780—1790 / *impressed*
174	**NYMPHENBURG** Kurfürstliche Porzellan- manufaktur 1850—1862 / *impressed*

175 **176**	**FRANKENTHAL** P. Hannong 1755—1759 / *blue*

177	**BLANKENHAIN** C. & A. Carstens 19th cent. / *blue*

178	**PIRKENHAMMER** (Březová) Fischer & Mieg after 1887—1890 / *gold*

179 **180** **181**	**BERLIN** Königliche Porzellanmanufaktur 1763—1780 / *blue*

182 **183**	**BERLIN** Königliche Porzellanmanufaktur 1780—1880 / *blue*

184	**BERLIN** Königliche Porzellanmanufaktur 1875—1944 / *blue*

185	**BERLIN** Königliche Porzellanmanufaktur 1847—1849 / *printed*

186	**BERLIN** Königliche Porzellanmanufaktur 1849—1870 / *printed*

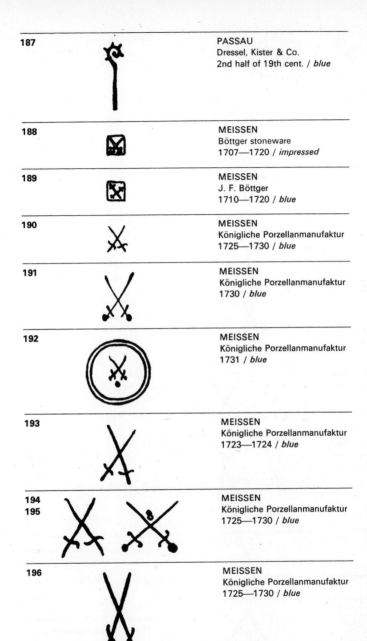

187

PASSAU
Dressel, Kister & Co.
2nd half of 19th cent. / *blue*

188

MEISSEN
Böttger stoneware
1707—1720 / *impressed*

189

MEISSEN
J. F. Böttger
1710—1720 / *blue*

190

MEISSEN
Königliche Porzellanmanufaktur
1725—1730 / *blue*

191

MEISSEN
Königliche Porzellanmanufaktur
1730 / *blue*

192

MEISSEN
Königliche Porzellanmanufaktur
1731 / *blue*

193

MEISSEN
Königliche Porzellanmanufaktur
1723—1724 / *blue*

194
195

MEISSEN
Königliche Porzellanmanufaktur
1725—1730 / *blue*

196

MEISSEN
Königliche Porzellanmanufaktur
1725—1730 / *blue*

197		MEISSEN Königliche Porzellanmanufaktur 1730—1735 / *blue*
198		MEISSEN Königliche Porzellanmanufaktur 1730—1740 / *blue*
199		MEISSEN Königliche Porzellanmanufaktur after 1750 / *blue*
200		MEISSEN Königliche Porzellanmanufaktur 1730—1740 / *blue*
201		MEISSEN Königliche Porzellanmanufaktur *c.* 1765 / *blue*
202 203		MEISSEN Königliche Porzellanmanufaktur after 1763 / *blue*
204 205		MEISSEN Königliche Porzellanmanufaktur after 1774 / *blue*
206		MEISSEN Königliche Porzellanmanufaktur 1772 and after 1774 / *blue*
207		MEISSEN Königliche Porzellanmanufaktur 1774—1830 / *impressed*

208		MEISSEN Königliche Porzellanmanufaktur beginning of 19th cent. / *blue*
209		MEISSEN Königliche Porzellanmanufaktur after 1723, with mark of Master Kretschner added / *blue*
210		MEISSEN Königliche Porzellanmanufaktur 1st half of 18th cent., with mark of Master Moebius / *blue*
211		MEISSEN Königliche Porzellanmanufaktur after 1766, medium quality *blue*
212		MEISSEN Königliche Porzellanmanufaktur after 1766, medium quality, unpainted / *blue*
213		MEISSEN Königliche Porzellanmanufaktur after 1766, medium quality, painted / *blue*
214		MEISSEN Königliche Porzellanmanufaktur after 1766, discarded, painted / *blue*
215		MEISSEN Königliche Porzellanmanufaktur after 1766, discarded, unpainted / *blue*
216		MEISSEN Königliche Porzellanmanufaktur after 1766, second quality, painted / *blue*
217		MEISSEN Königliche Porzellanmanufaktur after 1766, third quality / *blue*

218	MEISSEN Königliche Porzellanmanufaktur after 1766, discarded / *blue*
219	MEISSEN Königliche Hofconditorei Warschau 1763—1806 / *black, red*
220	MEISSEN Königliche Porzellanmanufaktur after 1724, with a number indicating the service / *blue*
221	MEISSEN Königliche Porzellanmanufaktur modellers' marks, 18th cent. *blue* Georg Kittel Peter Geithner Gottfried Lohse Johann Christoph Krumbholtz Johann Donner Johann Kittel Christoph Busch Johann Meisel Georg Michel Johann Michal Schuhmann
222	VOLKSTEDT-RUDOLSTADT C. Nonne after 1788—1799 / *blue*
223	LOWESTOFT imitation of Meissen mark 18th cent. / *blue*
224	CHELSEA imitations of Meissen 18th cent. / *blue, gold*
225	WEESP Count Gronsveldt-Diepenbroek 1759—1771 / *blue*

226		**WEESP** Count Gronsveldt-Diepenbroek 1759—1771 / *blue*
227		**BRISTOL** R. Champion end of 18th cent. / *blue, incised*
228		**BRISTOL** R. Champion end of 18th cent. / *blue, incised*
229		**BRISTOL** R. Champion end of 18th cent. / *blue, incised*
230		**BRISTOL** R. Champion end of 18th cent. / *blue, incised*
231		**BRISTOL** R. Champion 1773—1781 / *blue, incised*
232		**WORCESTER** Dr Wall 1751—1783 / *blue*
233		**DERBY** imitations of Meissen middle of 18th cent. / *blue*
234		**TOURNAI** F. J. Peterinck 1763—1800 / *blue, gold*

235		KÖPPELSDORF J. Hering & Sohn *c.* 1893 / *printed*
236		FREIWALDAU (Gozdnica) H. Schmidt 2nd half of 19th cent. / *printed*
237		VINCENNES Séguin factory, coat of arms of the duke of Chartres after 1777—1788 / *blue*
238		ORLÉANS Manufacture Royale de porce- layne d'Orléans 1767—1806 / *blue*
239		PARIS, RUE DE LA ROQUETTE J. V. Dubois after 1774 / *blue*
240		EISENBERG Porzellanfabrik Kalk G. m. b. H. after 1900 / *blue*
241		MITTERTEICH M. Emanuel & Co. after 1900 / *printed*
242		BOW Weatherby & Crowther *c.* 1750 / *blue*
243		WORCESTER Wall period 1751—1783 / *blue*
244		BOW Weatherby & Crowther *c.* 1750 / *incised*

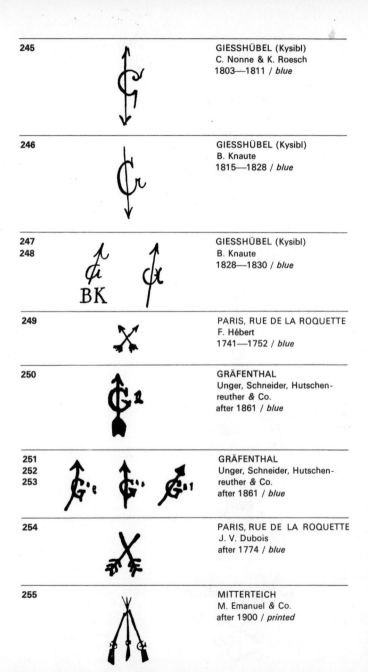

245

GIESSHÜBEL (Kysibl)
C. Nonne & K. Roesch
1803—1811 / *blue*

246

GIESSHÜBEL (Kysibl)
B. Knaute
1815—1828 / *blue*

247
248

GIESSHÜBEL (Kysibl)
B. Knaute
1828—1830 / *blue*

249

PARIS, RUE DE LA ROQUETTE
F. Hébert
1741—1752 / *blue*

250

GRÄFENTHAL
Unger, Schneider, Hutschenreuther & Co.
after 1861 / *blue*

251
252
253

GRÄFENTHAL
Unger, Schneider, Hutschenreuther & Co.
after 1861 / *blue*

254

PARIS, RUE DE LA ROQUETTE
J. V. Dubois
after 1774 / *blue*

255

MITTERTEICH
M. Emanuel & Co.
after 1900 / *printed*

256		CHELSEA Triangle period (Sprimont-Gouyn) 1745—1750 / *blue*
257 258		PARIS, RUE FONTAINE AU ROY L. Russinger after 1771 / *blue*
259		PARIS, RUE FONTAINE AU ROY Pouyat after 1800 / *blue*
260 261		VOLKSTEDT-RUDOLSTADT C. Nonne 1787—1799 / *blue*
262		VOLKSTEDT-RUDOLSTADT C. Nonne 1808—1890 / *blue*
263		VOLKSTEDT-RUDOLSTADT C. Nonne 1808—1890 / *blue*
264 265		VOLKSTEDT-RUDOLSTADT R. Eckert & Co. after 1895—after 1900 *printed*
266		VOLKSTEDT-RUDOLSTADT R. Eckert & Co. after 1895—after 1900 / *printed*
267 268		PARIS, FAUBOURG SAINT DENIS Pierre A. Hannong 1771—1776 / *blue*
269		KÖPPELSDORF-NORD Schoenau Bros, Swaine & Co. after 1854 / *blue*

270 **271**	**ARNSTADT** Porzellanfabrik after 1790 / *blue*
272	**SCEAUX** J. Jullien & S. Jacques 1763—1772 / *incised*
273 **274**	**VENICE** G. Cozzi 1766—1813 / *red, gold*
275	**CHELSEA** Anchor period (Sprimont-Fawkener) after 1753—1758 / *red*
276	**CHELSEA** Anchor period (Sprimont-Fawkener) after 1753—1758 / *blue*
277	**CHELSEA** Anchor period (Sprimont-Fawkener) after 1750—1753 / *red*
278	**BOW** W. Duesbury 1760—1766 / *red*
279 **280**	**SCHWARZENBACH** O. Schaller & Co. after 1882 / *printed*
281	**BARANOVKA** Mezer Bros 1804—1850 / *blue*
282	**BOW** W. Duesbury 1760—1776 / *red*
283	**BOW** W. Duesbury 1760—1776 / *blue, red*
284	**BOW** W. Duesbury 1760—1776 / *red*

285		BOW W. Duesbury 1760—1776 / *red*

286		CHELSEA Raised Anchor period 1750—1753 / *impressed*

287		HÖCHST Kurfürstliche Porzellan- manufaktur 1758—1765 / *impressed*

288 289		HÖCHST Kurfürstliche Porzellan- manufaktur 1750—1763 / *red, black, brown* / *blue*

290		HÖCHST Kurfürst Emmerich von Breiden- bach 1765—1774 / *blue*

291		PASSAU imitations of Höchst 19th cent. / *blue*

292 293		DAMM casts from Höchst's models 1860—1888 / *blue*

294		DAMM casts from Höchst's models 1840—1845 / *blue*

295		DAMM casts from Höchst's models 1850—1860 / *blue*

296		DAMM casts from Höchst's models 19th cent. / *blue*

297	CHANTILLY Prince de Condé 1726—1740 / *blue, red*
298	CHANTILLY Prince de Condé 1740—1800 / *blue*
299	CHANTILLY Prince de Condé 1740—1800 / *bleu*
300	ALT-ROHLAU (Stará Role) F. Manka from 1883 / *printed*
301	OHRDRUF Kling & Co. 1836—1941 / *printed*
302	VIENNA M. G. Grossbaum 1889 / *blue*
303	ALT-HALDENSLEBEN Schmerzer & Gericke 2nd half of 19th cent. / *printed*
304	ALT-ROHLAU (Stará Role) M. Zdekauer after 1884 / *printed*
305	DELFT Ary de Milde end of 17th cent. / *impressed*

306		**LORCH** Deusch & Co. after 1898 / *printed*
307		**MITTERTEICH** M. Emanuel & Co. end of 19th cent. / *printed*
308		**ILMENAU** Metzler Bros & Ortloff after 1876 / *printed*
309		**SCHEDEWITZ** A. Unger 20th cent. / *printed*
310	 	**STADTLENGSFELD** Porzellanfabrik A. G. *c.* 1900 / *printed*
311		**DOCCIA** R. Ginori 18th cent. / *blue*
312		**KÖPPELSDORF** E. Heubach after 1887 / *blue*
313		**STADTLENGSFELD** Porzellanfabrik A. G. *c.* 1920 / *printed*

314		TOURNAI F. J. Peterinck 1753—1780 / *blue, gold*
315		TOURNAI F. J. Peterinck 1753—1780 / *gold*
316		TOURNAI F. J. Peterinck 1753—1780 / *red, violet*
317		TOURNAI F. J. Peterinck 1753—1780 / *gold*
318		TOURNAI F. J. Peterinck 1752—1762 / *various colours*
319 320		TOURNAI F. J. Peterinck 1752—1762 / *various colours*
321		TOURNAI F. J. Peterinck 1752—1762 / *various colours*
322		PARIS, CLIGNANCOURT P. Deruelle after 1771—1775 / *gold*
323		PARIS, CLIGNANCOURT P. Deruelle after 1771—1775 / *red*
324		MANTUA, CANETTO SULL'OGLIO Ceramica Furga after 1872 / *printed*

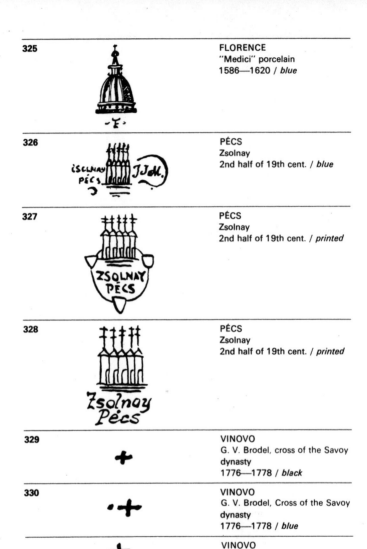

325	FLORENCE "Medici" porcelain 1586—1620 / *blue*
326	PÉCS Zsolnay 2nd half of 19th cent. / *blue*
327	PÉCS Zsolnay 2nd half of 19th cent. / *printed*
328	PÉCS Zsolnay 2nd half of 19th cent. / *printed*
329	VINOVO G. V. Brodel, cross of the Savoy dynasty 1776—1778 / *black*
330	VINOVO G. V. Brodel, Cross of the Savoy dynasty 1776—1778 / *blue*
	VINOVO G. V. Brodel 1776—1778 / *blue*
332	VINOVO Dr V. A. Gioanetti after 1780 until 1815 / *blue*

333		**VINOVO** Porcelain factory, with the mark of the painter Carasso before 1820 / *blue*
334		**FULDA** city arms 1765—1775 / *blue*
335		**BRISTOL** R. Champion 1773—1781 / *blue*
336		**BRISTOL** R. Champion 1773—1781 / *blue*
337		**PLYMOUTH** W. Cookworthy after 1768—1770 / *blue or* *incised*
338		**BOURG LA REINE** J. Jullien & S. Jacques after 1773—1804 / *blue*
339		**SITZENDORF** Voigt Bros after 1850 / *blue*
340		**BERLIN** Royal Porcelain Factory from 1870 / *printed*
341		**COPENHAGEN** F. H. Müller after 1773 / *impressed*

342	PLAUE C. G. Schierholz & Sohn after 1817 / *blue*
343 344	PLAUE C. G. Schierholz & Sohn after 1817 / *blue*
345	SITZENDORF Voigt Bros after 1850 / *blue*
346	WORCESTER Mark of a painter from the Wall period 1751—1783 / *blue*
347	MARIEBERG H. Sten 1769—1788 / *blue*
348	BOW W. Duesbury 1760—1776 / *blue*
349 350	KORZEC Czartoryski-Mezer 1790—1797 / *gold*
351	CHELSEA Triangle period 1745—1749 / *incised*
352	CHELSEA Triangle period 1745—1749 / *printed*
353	WORCESTER Wall period 1751—1783 / *blue*
354 355 356	WORCESTER Wall period 1751—1783 / *blue*
357	WORCESTER Wall period 1751—1783 / *blue*
358	WORCESTER Wall period 1751—1783 / *blue*

359		MOSCOW Kudinov 19th cent. / *blue*
360	*A*	ALCORA Count Aranda—P. Cloostermans after 1786 / *brown, black*
361	*A*	ALCORA Count Aranda—P. Cloostermans after 1786 / *gold*
362	*A*	ALCORA Count Aranda—P. Cloostermans after 1786 / *incised*
363	*A*	BOW 3rd period, W. Duesbury 1760—1776 / *blue*
364	*A*	LONGTON HALL W. Littler 1750—1760 / *blue*
365	*A*	PARIS, RUE THIROUX A. M. Lebœuf 1776—1790 / *blue, red*
366	A	AICH (Doubí) J. Möhling 1849—1860 / *impressed*
367	A	TURN (Trnovany) Riessner & Kessel after 1892 / *printed*
368	*A*	ANSBACH Markgräfliche Porzellanmanufaktur after 1758 / *blue*
369	*A*	ANSBACH Markgräfliche Porzellanmanufaktur after 1758 / *blue*

370 371 372		ANSBACH Markgräfliche Porzellan- manufaktur after 1758 / *blue*
373		ANSBACH Markgräfliche Porzellan- manufaktur after 1758 / *blue*
374		SITZERODE G. H. Macheleid middle of 18th cent. / *blue*
375		ANSBACH Markgräfliche Porzellan- manufaktur *c.* 1765 / *blue*
376		ANSBACH Markgräfliche Porzellan- manufaktur *c.* 1765 / *blue*
377		ANSBACH Markgräfliche Porzellan- manufaktur *c.* 1765 / *blue*
378		ANSBACH mark of the palace porcelain 1757—1790 / *blue*
379		ANSBACH mark of the palace porcelain 1757—1790 / *blue*
380		ANSBACH mark of the palace porcelain 1757—1790 / *blue*

381 **382**	**PARIS, RUE THIROUX** Manufacture de la Reine Marie Antoinette 1776—1790 / *blue, red*
383	**WEIDEN** A. Bauscher after 1881 / *blue*
384 	**ELGERSBURG** E. & F. C. Arnoldi second half of 19th cent. / *blue*
385 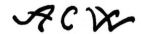	**BAYREUTH** painter A. C. Wanderer 1727—1748 / *blue*
386	**ARZBERG** C. Schumann after 1881 / *printed*
387	**PARIS, GROS CAILLOU** Advenier & Lamare 1773—1784 / *blue*
388	**LONGTON** Adderley Watership end of 18th cent. / *printed*
389	**LONGTON** Adderley Watership beginning of 19th cent. *printed*

390		LONGTON Adderley Watership 19th cent. / *printed*
391		ILMENAU A. Fischer 1907 / *printed*
392		ILMENAU A. Fischer 1907 / *printed*
393		VIERZON H. Hachez & Co. 19th cent. / *printed*
394		AICH (Doubí) J. Möhling 1849 — 1860 / *impressed*
395		BUDAU (Budov) A. Lang 1860—1880 / *impressed*
396		LONGTON Royal Albert Bone China after 1844 / *printed*
397		LONGTON Royal Albert Bone China after 1844 / *printed*

398 *Robert Allen 1760*	LOWESTOFT R. Allen after 1780 / *blue*
399 *Allen Lowestoft*	LOWESTOFT R. Allen after 1780 / *blue*
400 *,Allen owestoft*	LOWESTOFT R. Allen after 1780 / *blue*
401	ALTENBURG 19th cent. / *printed*
402 **ALTON BONE CHINA**	LONGTON Alton China after 1950 / *printed*
403	ALT-ROHLAU (Stará Role) B. Hasslacher 1813—1824 / *impressed*
404	ALT-ROHLAU (Stará Role) A. Nowotny 1838—1884 / *impressed*
405	ALT-ROHLAU (Stará Role) M. Zdekauer 1884—1920 / *printed*

| 406 | MZ Altrohlau CMR CZECHOSLOVAKIA | ALT-ROHLAU (Stará Role) M. Zdekauer after 1920 / *printed* |

| 407 | NOWOTNY IN ALTENROHLAU BEY KARLSBAD | ALT-ROHLAU (Stará Role) A. Nowotny 1838—1884 / *printed* |

| 408 | C. TIELSCH & C° ALTWASSER | WALDENBURG (Walbrzych) C. Tielsch 1845—1948 / *printed* |

| 409 | C.T. ALTWASSER | WALDENBURG (Walbrzych) C. Tielsch *c.* 1900 / *printed* |

| 410 | C.T. ALTWASSER | WALDENBURG (Walbrzych) C. Tielsch *c.* 1900 / *printed* |

| 411 | A M | AICH (Doubí) J. Möhling *c.* 1860 / *impressed* |

| 412 | A M | AICH (Doubí) J. Möhling before 1860 / *impressed* |

| 413 | A M | KÖPPELSDORF-NORD A. Marseille after 1887 / *printed* |

| 414 | A M | KÖPPELSDORF-NORD A. Marseille after 1887 / *blue* |

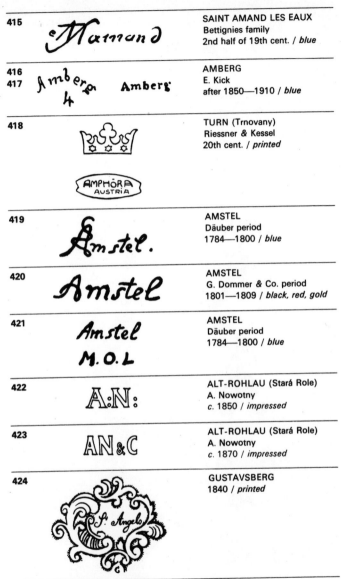

415

SAINT AMAND LES EAUX
Bettignies family
2nd half of 19th cent. / *blue*

416
417

AMBERG
E. Kick
after 1850—1910 / *blue*

418

TURN (Trnovany)
Riessner & Kessel
20th cent. / *printed*

419

AMSTEL
Däuber period
1784—1800 / *blue*

420

AMSTEL
G. Dommer & Co. period
1801—1809 / *black, red, gold*

421

AMSTEL
Däuber period
1784—1800 / *blue*

422

ALT-ROHLAU (Stará Role)
A. Nowotny
c. 1850 / *impressed*

423

ALT-ROHLAU (Stará Role)
A. Nowotny
c. 1870 / *impressed*

424

GUSTAVSBERG
1840 / *printed*

425

SAINT CLOUD / ROUEN?
P. Chicaneau
end of 17th cent. / *blue*

426 427		SAINT CLOUD / ROUEN? P. Chicaneau end of 17th cent. / *blue*
428		UNTERWEISSBACH A. Porzelius middle of 19th cent. / *printed*
429		MEISSEN Augustus Rex 1723—1736 / *blue*
430		MEISSEN Augustus Rex 1723—1736 / *blue*
431		MEISSEN Augustus Rex 1723—1736 / *blue*
432 433	AR AR	ARRAS J. F. Boussemart & Delemer 1770—1790 / *red*
434	AR	ARRAS J. F. Boussemart & Delemer 1770—1790 / *blue*
435	delé AR 2 o	ARRAS Delemer 1772—1790 / *blue*
436	A.R P	ARRAS Delemer 1772—1790 / *blue*

437		MILAN A. Richard after 1850 / *blue*
438		COPENHAGEN A. Mollert 18th cent. / *impressed*
439		ELBOGEN (Loket) R. E. Haidinger imitations of Meissen 19th cent. / *blue*
440		WEIDEN Bauscher Bros after 1881 / *printed*
441		KÖNIGSZELT (Jaworzyna Śląska) A. Rosenthal & Co. *c.* 1900 / *printed*
442		ALT-ROHLAU (Stará Role) M. Zdekauer after 1880 / *printed*
443		HELSINKI "Arabia" after 1948 / *printed*
444		HELSINKI "Arabia" after 1948 / *printed*

445		**HELSINKI** "Arabia" after 1948 / *printed*
446	**ARABIA**	**HELSINKI** "Arabia" after 1948 / *printed*
447		**DELFT** Ary de Milde *c.* 1700 / *impressed*
448		**ARZBERG** a branch of the Kahl porcelain factory after 1890 / *printed*
449		**ARZBERG** C. M. Hutschenreuther after 1839 / *printed*
450		**ARZBERG** C. M. Hutschenreuther 2nd half of 19th cent. / *printed*
451 452		**LONGTON** Aynsley China 1st half of 19th cent. / *printed*
453		**SAINT AMAND LES EAUX** M. Bettignies 1st half of 19th cent. / *blue*

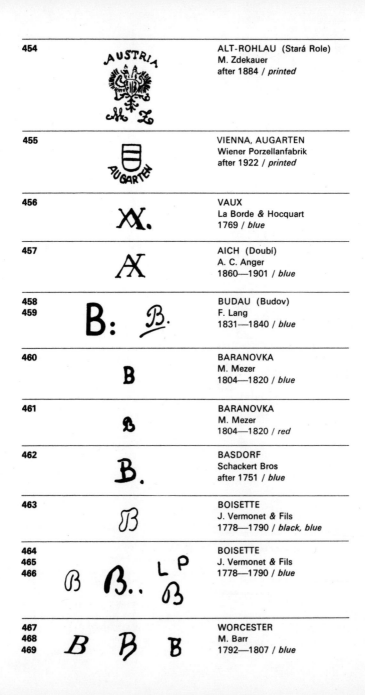

454		ALT-ROHLAU (Stará Role) M. Zdekauer after 1884 / *printed*
455		VIENNA, AUGARTEN Wiener Porzellanfabrik after 1922 / *printed*
456		VAUX La Borde & Hocquart 1769 / *blue*
457		AICH (Doubí) A. C. Anger 1860—1901 / *blue*
458 459		BUDAU (Budov) F. Lang 1831—1840 / *blue*
460		BARANOVKA M. Mezer 1804—1820 / *blue*
461		BARANOVKA M. Mezer 1804—1820 / *red*
462		BASDORF Schackert Bros after 1751 / *blue*
463		BOISETTE J. Vermonet & Fils 1778—1790 / *black, blue*
464 465 466		BOISETTE J. Vermonet & Fils 1778—1790 / *blue*
467 468 469		WORCESTER M. Barr 1792—1807 / *blue*

470		BOW W. Duesbury 1760—1776 / *blue, red*
471		BOW T. Frye 1755—1760 / *blue*
472		LASSAY L. L. F. Comte de Lauraguais- Brancas 1763—1768 / *incised*
473		BRUSSELS J. S. Vaume 1786—1790 / *blue, red*
474		BRUSSELS, SCHAERBEEK J. S. Vaume 1786—1790 / *blue, red*
475 476		BRISTOL W. Cookworthy 1773—1781 / *blue*
477		RUDOLSTADT E. Bohne from 1854 / *blue*
478		BARANOVKA M. Mezer after 1805 / *blue, gold*
479 480		BARANOVKA M. Mezer after 1805 / *red*
481		BARANOVKA M. Mezer after 1805—1825 / *red*
482		BARANOVKA M. Mezer after 1805—1825 / *blue*

483 484	*Boranowka* **B**	BARANOVKA M. Mezer after 1805—1825 / *black*
485	*Baranouka*	BARANOVKA M. Mezer after 1805—1825 / *black*
486	*Basdorf*	BASDORF Schackert Bros after 1751 / *blue*
487	Bavaria	PLANKENHAMMER after 1908 / *printed*
488	BAVARIA	WALDSASSEN Bayreuther & Co. after 1866 / *printed*
489	A C S BAVARIA	ARZBERG C. Schumann after 1881 / *printed*
490	GKC BAVARIA	WALDSASSEN Gareis, Kühnl & Co. after 1899 / *printed*
491	BAVARIA G·K·Co	WALDSASSEN Gareis, Kühnl & Co. after 1899 / *printed*
492	G.M.O BAVARIA	WALDSASSEN Gareis, Kühnl & Co. after 1899 / *printed*

493		MARKTLEUTHEN H. Winterling after 1903 / *printed*
494		ERKERSREUTH Hoffmann Bros 20th cent. / *printed*
495		SCHWARZENBACH J. Kronester & Co. after 1904 / *printed*
496		MITTERTEICH Porzellanfabrik A. G. after 1917 / *printed*
497		MARKTREDWITZ Jaeger & Co. after 1872 / *printed*
498		SELB P. Müller 1890—1912 / *printed*
499		WUNSIEDEL Retsch & Co. after 1885 / *printed*
500		RÖSLAU Winterling Bros after 1906 / *printed*

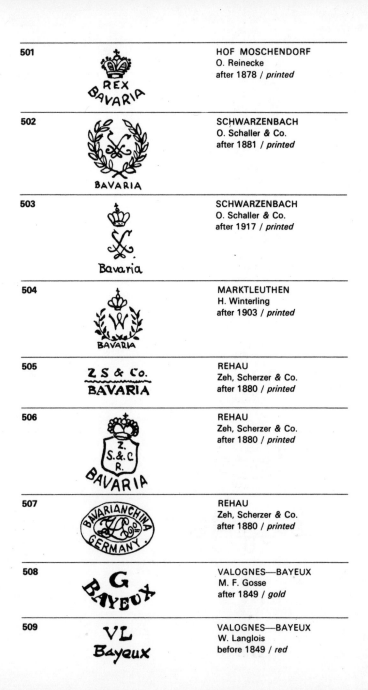

501	HOF MOSCHENDORF O. Reinecke after 1878 / *printed*
502	SCHWARZENBACH O. Schaller & Co. after 1881 / *printed*
503	SCHWARZENBACH O. Schaller & Co. after 1917 / *printed*
504	MARKTLEUTHEN H. Winterling after 1903 / *printed*
505	REHAU Zeh, Scherzer & Co. after 1880 / *printed*
506	REHAU Zeh, Scherzer & Co. after 1880 / *printed*
507	REHAU Zeh, Scherzer & Co. after 1880 / *printed*
508	VALOGNES—BAYEUX M. F. Gosse after 1849 / *gold*
509	VALOGNES—BAYEUX W. Langlois before 1849 / *red*

510	VALOGNES—BAYEUX M. F. Gosse after 1849 / *red*
511	SOPHIENTHAL Thomas & Co. after 1948 / *printed*
512 	SOPHIENTHAL Thomas & Co. 1928—1934 / *printed*
513	BAYREUTH S. P. Meyer, "Walküre" after 1900 / *printed*
514	WALDSASSEN Bayreuther & Co. after 1866 / *printed*
515 **Bayswater**	BAYSWATER English paint-room of Chinese and European porcelain 18th —19th cent. / *printed*
516	EICHWALD (Dubí) Bloch & Co. after 1871 / *blue*
517 **BB**	EICHWALD (Dubí) Bloch & Co. after 1871 / *blue*

518	B. D. J	SAINT AMAND LES EAUX J. B. Fauquez 1771—1778 / *blue*
519	FINE BONE *Bell* CHINA ENGLAND	LONGTON Shore & Coggins Ltd 19th cent. / *printed*
520	FINE BONE *Bell China* MADE IN ENGLAND	LONGTON Shore & Coggins Ltd 19th cent. / *printed*
521	BELLEEK	BELLEEK D. Birnay after 1863 / *printed*
522	BEM	MAGDEBURG-BUCKAU Buckauer Porzellanmanufaktur after 1832 / *blue*
523	BFB	WORCESTER Barr, Flight & Barr 1807—1813 / *impressed*
524	B.F.B.	WORCESTER Barr, Flight & Barr 1807—1813 / *blue*
525	B & G	COPENHAGEN Bing & Grøndahl 1854—1864 / *blue*
526	B·G DENMP DANISH CHINA WORKS B & G	COPENHAGEN Bing & Grøndahl after 1854—1864 / *blue*

527		**COPENHAGEN** Bing & Grøndahl after 1854—1864 / *blue*

527

COPENHAGEN
Bing & Grøndahl
after 1854—1864 / *blue*

528

MAYERHÖFEN
Benedikt Bros
1931—1945 / *printed*

529

LILLE
F. & B. Dorez
1720—1730 / *blue*

530

BK

GIESSHÜBEL (Kysibl)
B. Knaute
1828—1840 / *blue*

531

REICHENSTEIN
M. Blanka
after 1831 / *blue*

532

B la R

BOURG LA REINE
J. Jullien & S. Jacques
after 1773—1804 / *impressed*

533

DERBY
R. Bloor
1811—1849 / *printed*

534

DERBY
R. Bloor
1811—1849 / *printed*

535

LE NOVE
Fabbrica Antonibon
1762—1763 / *various colours, gold*

536	**NIDERVILLER** J. L. de Beyerlé 1765—1770 / *red*
537	**NIDERVILLER** J. L. de Beyerlé 1765—1770 / *blue*
538	**NEU-ROHLAU** (Nová Role) "Bohemia" 1921 / *printed*
539	**NEU-ROHLAU** (Nová Role) "Bohemia" 1921 / *printed*
540	**VIENNA** G. Mladenof & Co. after 1929 / *printed*
541 	**FENTON** A. Bowker 19th cent. / *printed*
542	**BORDEAUX** D. Johnston 1836—1845 / *violet*
543	**LONGTON** Cartwright & Edwards Ltd. after 1858 / *printed*

544	PARIS, RUE DE CRUSSOL C. Potter 1792—1800 / *blue*

$$\text{B}$$
$$\text{Potter}$$
$$\text{42}$$

545	BORDEAUX Verneuilh & Alluaud 1781—1790 / *impressed*

546	BOURG LA REINE J. Jullien & S. Jacques after 1773—1804 / *impressed*

B . R .

547	BOURG LA REINE J. Jullien & S. Jacques after 1773—1804 / *impressed*

B R
N

548	SWINTON Rockingham Factory 19th cent. / *printed*

BRAMELD

549	BOURNEMOUTH Branksome Ceramics after 1945 / *printed*

Branksome
China
England

550	BRISTOL R. Champion 1773—1781 / *red*

Bristolr

551	BRISTOL Putney & Co. after 1852 / *printed*

Bristol
Founded ✕ in 1652
England

552 	BRUSSELS, ETTERBEEK L. Demeuldre-Coché 1920—1930 / *printed*
553	BRUSSELS, ETTERBEEK L. Demeuldre-Coché 1920—1941 / *printed*
554 	BRUSSELS, ETTERBEEK L. Demeuldre-Coché 1920—1941 / *printed*
555 	BRUSSELS, ETTERBEEK Etablissements Demeuldre 20th cent. / *printed*
556 L.C Brux	BRUSSELS L. Cretté 1791—1803 / *red*
557 	BUDAPEST E. Fischer after 1868 / *printed*

558		**SHELTON** Brow, Westerheat & Co. after 1858 / *printed*
559	**C**	**CAUGHLEY** T. Turner after 1772—1783 / *blue*
560	*C*	**CHODAU** (Chodov) Hüttner & Co. 1835—1840 / *blue, gold*
561	*C*	**CHODAU** (Chodov) Haas & Czjizek after 1905 / *blue*
562	C	**CHODZIEŻ** Fabryka porcelany after 1882 / *blue*
563	Ć	**ĆMIELÓW** X. Drucko-Lubecki after 1842 / *blue*
564	CA	**UHLSTÄDT** R. Albert after 1873 / *blue*
565	FRANCE / DÉPOSÉ	**LIMOGES** C. Ahrenfeld after 1894 / *printed*
566	CA	**LIMOGES** C. Ahrenfeld end of 19th cent. / *printed*
567	**CAEN**	**CAEN** d'Aigmont-Desmares 1793—1806 / *red*
568	**caen**	**CAEN** d'Aigmont-Desmares 1793—1806 / *red*

569	CARLSBAD	FISCHERN (Rybáře) C. Knoll 1848—1868 / *impressed*
570		DELFT J. Caluve before 1730 / *impressed*
571	 ESTd. 1774 **CAULDON CHINA** ENGLAND	SHELTON Cauldon China 20th cent. / *printed*
572	C B D	COALPORT (COALBROOKDALE) after 1780 / *blue*
573	c͡ͅB	COALPORT (COALBROOKDALE) after 1780 / *blue*
574	G	COALPORT (COALBROOKDALE) after 1780 / *blue*
575	₿	COALPORT (COALBROOKDALE) after 1780 / *blue, gold*
576	C B DALE	COALPORT (COALBROOKDALE) after 1780 / *blue, gold*
577	X	NIDERVILLER A. P. de Custine 1770—1793 / *black*
578	X	LUDWIGSBURG Carl Eugen of Württemberg 1759—1793 / *blue*

579		LUDWIGSBURG Carl Eugen of Württemberg 1759—1793 / *blue*
580		NIDERVILLER A. P. de Custine 1770—1793 / *blue*
581		NIDERVILLER A. P. de Custine 1770—1793 / *blue*
582		LUDWIGSBURG Carl Eugen of Württemberg 1759—1793 / *blue*
583		LUDWIGSBURG Carl Eugen of Württemberg 1759—1806 / *blue*
584		LUDWIGSBURG Carl Eugen of Württemberg 1759—1806 / *blue*
585		ROME F. Cuccumos 1761—1781 / *blue*
586		SCHORNDORF C. M. Bauer & Pfeiffer after 1904—1939 / *printed*
587		COALPORT (COALBROOKDALE) after 1780 / *blue*
588		LIMOGES Grellet Frères after 1771—1796 / *blue, impressed, red, gold*

589	**LIMOGES** Grellet Frères after 1771—1796 / *blue, impressed, red, gold*
590	**LIMOGES** Grellet Frères after 1771—1796 / *blue, impressed, red, gold*
591	**LIMOGES** Grellet Frères 1771—1796 / *blue*
592	**SORAU (Żary)** C. & E. Carstens after 1918 / *printed*
593	**WÜRZBURG** C. Geyger 1775—1780 / *impressed*
594	**ZWICKAU** C. Fischer after 1850 / *blue*
595	**PIRKENHAMMER (Březová)** C. Fischer 1846—1857 / *impressed*
596	**MILAN** San Cristoforo 1830—1833 / *blue*
597	**WORCESTER** J. & J. Flight 1783—1791 / *red, blue*
598	**PARIS, BARRIÈRE DE REUILLY** H. F. Chanou 1779—1785 / *red, gold*
599	**WORCESTER** R. Chamberlain after 1840 / *blue*
600	**WORCESTER** Chamberlains after 1840 / *printed*

601

WORCESTER
R. Chamberlain
c. 1850 / *blue*

602

WORCESTER
Chamberlains
1852—1862 / *printed*

603

CHAMBERLAIN & CO.
WORCESTER
155 NEW BOND STREET
& NO. 1
COVENTRY St
LONDON.

WORCESTER
Chamberlains
1840—1845 / *printed*

604

WORCESTER
Chamberlains
1840—1845 / *printed*

605

WORCESTER
Chamberlains
1840—1845 / *printed*

606

CHAMBERLAINS

WORCESTER
Chamberlains
from 1840 / *printed*

607

STOKE-ON-TRENT
Mintons Ltd
from 1911 / *printed*

608

CHANTILLY
Prince de Condé
1760—1800 / *blue*

609	*chatillon*	**CHATILLON** Porcelain factory after 1775 / *blue*
610	**D⚓V** **Chatillon**	**CHATILLON** Porcelain factory after 1775 / *blue*
611	△ *Chelsea 1745*	**CHELSEA** N. Sprimont & C. Gouyn 1745—1749 / *incised*
612	Chodau	**CHODAU** (Chodov) Haas & Czjizek after 1920 / *impressed*
613	CHODAU H C CZJIZEK	**CHODAU** (Chodov) Haas & Czjizek after 1920 / *printed*
614	CHODAU H C CZECHOSLOVAKIA	**CHODAU** (Chodov) Haas & Czjizek after 1920 / *printed*
615	Porcelit Chodzież P	**CHODZIEŻ** Fabryka porcelany after 1882 / *printed*
616	C CHODZIEŻ	**CHODZIEŻ** Fabryka porcelany after 1882 / *printed*
617	CGF	**MANTUA,** **CANETTO SULL'OGLIO** Ceramica Furga after 1872 / *blue*
618	CL	**NIDERVILLER** C. Lanfrey 1792—1827 / *blue*
619	CL	**NIDERVILLER** C. Lanfrey 1792—1827 / *blue*

620		HOHENBERG C. M. Hutschenreuther 1865 / *printed*
621		ĆMIELÓW Fabryka porcelany 1842—1863 / *blue*
622		NIDERVILLER A. P. de Custine 1770—1802 / *blue*
623		NIDERVILLER A. P. de Custine 1770—1802 / *blue*
624		COALPORT Coalport China 2nd half of 19th cent. / *blue*
625		COALPORT Coalport China 1st half of 20th cent. / *printed*
626		COALPORT Coalport China 20th cent. / *printed*
627		COALPORT Coalport China 20th cent. / *printed*
628		HANLEY Booths & Colclough Ltd. 20th cent. / *printed*

629		HANLEY Booths & Colclough Ltd. 20th cent. / *printed*
630		HANLEY Booths & Colclough Ltd. 20th cent. / *printed*
631		LONGTON Collingwood Bros Ltd. 20th cent. / *printed*
632		STOKE-ON-TRENT W. T. Copeland after 1829—20th cent. / *blue*
633		STOKE-ON-TRENT W. T. Copeland after 1829—20th cent. / *blue*
634	**Copeland late Spode**	STOKE-ON-TRENT W. T. Copeland 1847—1867 / *blue*
635		STOKE-ON-TRENT W. T. Copeland after 1870 / *blue*
636	SPODE COPELANDS CHINA ENGLAND	STOKE-ON-TRENT W. T. Copeland 1847—1867 / *blue*
637	Copeland Stone China	STOKE-ON-TRENT W. T. Copeland 1847—1867 / *blue*
638		STOKE-ON-TRENT W. T. Copeland 20th cent. / *printed*

639		STOKE-ON-TRENT W. T. Copeland 20th cent. / *printed*
640		STOKE-ON-TRENT W. T. Copeland & Garrett 1833—1846 / *printed*
641		STOKE-ON-TRENT W. T. Copeland & Garrett 1833—1846 / *printed*
642		STOKE-ON-TRENT W. T. Copeland & Garrett 1833—1846 / *printed*
643		STOKE-ON-TRENT W. T. Copeland & Garrett 1833—1846 / *printed*
644		STOKE-ON-TRENT W. T. Copeland & Garrett 1833—1846 / *printed*
645		STOKE-ON-TRENT W. T. Copeland & Garrett 1833—1846 / *printed*
646		STOKE-ON-TRENT W. T. Copeland & Garrett 1833—1846 / *printed*

647 	STOKE-ON-TRENT W. T. Copeland & Garrett 1833—1846 / *printed*
648 COPELAND & GARRETT	STOKE-ON-TRENT W. T. Copeland & Garrett 1833—1846 / *printed*
649	COBURG A. Riemann after 1860/*printed*
650	CREIDLITZ Porzellanfabrik A. G. after 1907 / *printed*
651 *crepy*	CRÉPY EN VALOIS L. F. Gaignepain & P. Bourgeois 1762—1767 / *incised*
652 D, C, P,	CRÉPY EN VALOIS L. F. Gaignepain & P. Bourgeois 1762—1767 / *incised*
653 c.p.	CRÉPY EN VALOIS L. F. Gaignepain & P. Bourgeois 1762—1767 / *incised*
654 **655** CP CP	PARIS, RUE FAUBOURG SAINT DENIS Comte d'Artois 1779—1793 / *blue, red*
656 CPM	ĆMIELÓW Fabryka porcelany c. 1850 / *blue*
657	COPENHAGEN Royal Porcelain Factory 1889 / *green*

658

COPENHAGEN
Dahl-Jensens Porcelaensfabrik
after 1925 / *green*

659

COPENHAGEN
Royal Porcelain Factory
1897 / *green*

660

COPENHAGEN
Royal Porcelain Factory
1923 / *green*

661

COPENHAGEN
Bing & Grøndahl
after 1854 / *blue*

662

COPENHAGEN
Bing & Grøndahl
1905 / *red, various colours*

663

COPENHAGEN
Bing & Grøndahl
1914 / *red, various colours*

664

SCHWARZA-SAALBAHN
E. & A. Müller
after 1890 / *blue*

665		BRUSSELS L. Cretté 1791—1803 / *blue*
666		BRUSSELS L. Cretté 1791—1803 / *red, brown*
667		BRUSSELS L. Cretté 1791—1803 / *red, brown*
668		BRUSSELS L. Cretté 1791—1803 / *red, brown*
669		COALPORT Caughley, Swansea, Nantgarw after 1861 / *blue*
670		WALDENBURG (Walbrzych) C. Tielsch after 1945 / *blue*
671		POTSCHAPPEL C. Thieme after 1872 / *blue*
672		WALDENBURG (Walbrzych) C. Tielsch after 1845 / *blue*
673		POTSCHAPPEL C. Thieme 20th cent. / *printed*

674	WALDENBURG (Walbrzych) C. Tielsch after 1845 / *blue*
675	KLOSTER VEILSDORF W. E. von Hildburghausen before 1765 / *blue*
676	KLOSTER VEILSDORF W. E. von Hildburghausen 1760—1797 / *blue*
677	KLOSTER VEILSDORF W. E. von Hildburghausen 1760—1797 / *blue*
678	SCHLACKENWERTH (Ostrov) Pfeiffer & Löwenstein after 1918 / *printed*
679	LUNÉVILLE P. L. Cyfflé 1766—1780 / *blue*
680	ALT-ROHLAU (Stará Role) M. Zdekauer after 1918 / *printed*
681 682	DERBY W. Duesbury & J. Heath 1770—1784 / *gold*
683	DERBY W. Duesbury & J. Heath after 1750 / *incised*
684	DERBY W. Duesbury & J. Heath 1770—1784 / *red, gold*
685	DERBY W. Duesbury & J. Heath 1770—1784 / *gold*

686	**DERBY** W. Duesbury & J. Heath 1784—1811 / *blue, red, gold*
687	**DERBY** W. Duesbury 1784—1810 / *incised*
688	**DERBY** W. Duesbury 1784—1810 / *blue, red*
689	**DERBY** R. Bloor 1811—1848 / *blue, red*
690	**DERBY** W. Duesbury 1784—1810 / *blue, red*
691	**DERBY** R. Bloor 1811—1848 / *printed, red*
692	**DERBY** Stevenson & Handcock 1850—1870 / *red*
693	**DRESDEN** 19th cent. / *blue*
694	**DALLWITZ** (Dalovice) V. W. Lorenz 1831—1850 / *impressed*

695		DUISDORF "Rhenania" after 1904 / *printed*
696		BRUSSELS, ETTERBEEK H. Demeuldre 20th cent. / *printed*
697		VINOVO G. Balbo c. 1800 / *red, green*
698		DALLWITZ (Dalovice) V. W. Lorenz 1832—1850 / *impressed*
699		STOKE-ON-TRENT Minton & Boyle 1836—1841 / *printed*
700		COALPORT (COALBROOKDALE) end of 18th cent. / *blue*
701	DALWITZ	DALLWITZ (Dalovice) V. W. Lorenz 1832—1850 / *impressed*
702	W.W.L. DALWITZ	DALLWITZ (Dalovice) V. W. Lorenz 1832—1850 / *impressed*
703	DAMM	DAMM Steingut- und Porzellanfabrik 1827—1884 / *impressed*

704	COPENHAGEN Royal Porcelain Factory 1894 / *green, blue*
705	PARIS, RUE DE CHARONNE Darte Frères *c.* 1800 / *red*
706	PARIS, RUE DE CHARONNE Darte Frères *c.* 1800 / *red*
707	LONGPORT Davenport 1793—1882 / *blue, printed*
708	LONGPORT Davenport 1793—1882 / *blue, printed*
709	WORCESTER Flight & Barr 1792—1807 / *incised*
710	COALPORT (COALBROOKDALE) *c.* 1850 / *blue*
711 **712**	PARIS, CLIGNANCOURT P. Deruelle 1775—1793 / *red*
713	CRÉPY EN VALOIS L. Gaignepain & L. Bourgeois 1762—1767 / *blue*
714	CRÉPY EN VALOIS L. Gaignepain & L. Bourgeois 1762—1767 / *blue*

715 delemer l'an 1771 AR

ARRAS
Delemer
1772—1790 / *blue*

716

COPENHAGEN
Royal Porcelain Factory
1890 / *red, green*

717

LONGTON
Denton China Company
20th cent. / *printed*

718

DERBY
A. Planché
1750 / *incised*

719

DERBY
W. Duesbury
after 1770—1784 / *red*

720

DERBY
R. Bloor
1850—1870 / *red*

721

DERBY
R. Bloor
1811—1849 / *blue, red*

722

DERBY
R. Bloor
1811—1849 / *red*

723

DERBY
Locker & Co.
1849—1870 / *red*

724	**DERBY** Stevenson, Sharp & Co. 1859 / *red*
725	**DERBY** W. Duesbury 1784—1810 / *red*
726	**DERBY** W. Duesbury 1784—1810 / *red*
727 	**VINOVO** Dr. V. A. Gioanetti after 1780 / *blue*
728 DH	**CHODAU** (Chodov) J. Hüttner & Co. 1835—1840 / *impressed*
729	**MARKTREDWITZ** Jaeger & Co. after 1872 / *printed*
730 	**LONGTON** A. T. Finney & Sons Ltd 20th cent. / *printed*
731	**PARIS, RUE DE BONDY** J. Dihl 1817—1829 / *blue, red*

732		DERBY W. Duesbury & M. Kean 1795—1796 / *blue, red*
733		DERBY W. Duesbury & M. Kean 1795—1796 / *red, blue*
734 735 736	DKF DKF DKF	GRÄFENRODA Dornheim, Koch & Fischer after 1860 / *blue*
737	DILLWYN & C° SWANSEA.	SWANSEA L. W. Dillwyn 1814—1850 / *printed*
738	DONATH T.	TIEFENFURTH (Parowa) P. Donath after 1883 / *printed*
739	*Donovan's* *Irish Manufactur*	DUBLIN Donovan & Son beginning of 19th cent. / *red*
740	Donovan's Irish Manufacture	DUBLIN Donovan & Son beginning of 19th cent. / *red, violet*
741	**Donovan** **Dublin**	DUBLIN Donovan & Son beginning of 19th cent. / *red*
742	DONOVAN 481	DUBLIN Donovan & Son beginning of 19th cent. / *blue*
743	DOULTON & C° LIMITED LAMBETH	BURSLEM Doulton & Co. after 1815 / *printed*

744

BURSLEM
Doulton & Co.
after 1815 / *printed*

745

BURSLEM
Doulton & Co.
after 1815 / *printed*

746

BURSLEM
Doulton & Co.
after 1815 / *printed*

747

DRESDEN
19th cent. / *blue*

748

KRONACH
P. Rosenthal & Co.
end of 19th cent. / *blue*

749

LONGTON
Dresden Floral Porcelain Co.
from 1845 / *printed*

750

DRESDEN
Dresdner Porzellanmanufaktur
20th cent. / *printed*

751	**POTSCHAPPEL** C. Thieme after 1872 / *printed*
752	**DRESDEN** Dresdner Porzellanmanufaktur 20th cent. / *printed*
	DRESDEN.
753	W.DUESBURY. 1803.	**DERBY** W. Duesbury 1803 / *red*
754	DUCHESS BONE CHINA MADE IN ENGLAND	**LONGTON** A. T. Finney & Sons Ltd 20th cent. / *printed*
755	DURHAM CHINA MADE IN ENGLAND	**GATESHEAD** Durham China Company 20th cent. / *printed*
756	Rhenania Duisdorf-Bonn	**DUISDORF** "Rhenania" after 1904 / *printed*
757	.D.V.	**MENNECY** Duc de Villeroy 1740—1773 / *incised*
758	.D.V.	**MENNECY** Duc de Villeroy 1734—1740 / *blue and other colours*

759 **D.V**	**MENNECY** Duc de Villeroy 1734—1740 / *blue, red, black,* *brown*
760	**MENNECY** Duc de Villeroy 1734—1740 / *red, blue, black,* *brown*
761 E	**EICHWALD** (Dubí) Bloch & Co. after 1871 / *blue*
762 E *Made in Czechoslovakia*	**EICHWALD** (Dubí) Bloch & Co. after 1920 / *blue*
763 ORIGINAL E.	**EICHWALD** (Dubí) Bloch & Co. c. 1900 / *blue*
764 E.	**EISENBERG** F. A. Reinecke after 1796 / *blue*
765 E Pelleve 1770	**ETIOLLES** D. Pellevé c. 1770 / *incised*
766 **ÉB**	**PARIS, RUE DE CRUSSOL** E. Blancheron 1792—1807 / *blue*
767 B S E	**EISENBERG** Bremer & Schmidt after 1895 / *printed*
768 DUROMA E	**DUX** (Duchcov) E. Eichler after 1860 / *printed*

769		DUX (Duchcov) E. Eichler *c.* 1900 / *printed*
770		POSCHETZAU (Božičany) Maier & Co. after 1890 / *printed*
771		EICHWALD (Dubí) Bloch & Co. after 1918 / *printed*
772		EICHWALD (Dubí) Bloch & Co. after 1871 / *printed*
773		EISENBERG W. Jäger after 1867 / *printed*
774		ELGERSBURG E. & F. C. Arnoldi after 1808 / *printed*
775		MERKELSGRÜN (Merklín) "Elsa" Porzellan 1900 until 1918 / *printed*
776		MIDDLETON *c.* 1870 / *printed*

777		**LONGTON** Cartwright & Edwards Ltd after 1858 / *printed*
778 **779**		**VOLKSTEDT-RUDOLSTADT** K. Ens after 1898 / *printed*
780		**AICH** (Doubí) "Epiag" after 1918 / *printed*
781		**ALT-ROHLAU** (Stará Role) "Epiag" after 1918 / *printed*
782		**TILLOWITZ** (Tulowice) Reinholdt & Schlegelmilch after 1869 / *printed*
783		**ERBENDORF** C. Seltmann after 1940 / *printed*
784		**ERBENDORF** C. Seltmann after 1940 / *printed*
785 **786**		**WINDISCH-ESCHENBACH** O. Schaller & Co. and successors after 1913 / *printed*
787		**STADTLENGSFELD** Porzellanfabrik A. G. *c.* 1900 / *printed*

788	*Eterbeek*	BRUSSELS, ETTERBEEK C. Kuhne 1787—1803 / *incised*
789	*Etiolle* *x bre 1770* *Pelleve*	ETIOLLES D. Pellevé c. 1770 / *incised*
790 791	*F* *J*	FÜRSTENBERG Charles I of Brunswick 1753—1770 / *blue*
792 793	*F* *F*	FÜRSTENBERG Charles I of Brunswick 1770—1800 / *blue*
794	*F*	FÜRSTENBERG Herzogliche Porzellan- manufaktur 20th cent. / *blue*
795	*F*	FÜRSTENBERG Herzogliche Porzellan- manufaktur 1800—1860 / *blue*
796	*F*	WORCESTER Dr Wall 1751—1783 / *blue*
797	*7 ..*	BOW T. Frye 1755—1760 / *blue*
798	*F*	PARIS, RUE DE LA PAIX J. Feuillet after 1820 / *green*
799	*F*	VOLKSTEDT-RUDOLSTADT E. Bohne 19th cent. / *blue*
800	*Ⓕ*	FRAUREUTH Römer & Födisch 2nd half of 19th cent. / *blue*

801	FRAUREUTH Römer & Födisch 2nd half of 19th cent. / *blue*
802	COPENHAGEN Royal Porcelain Factory (monogram of Frederick V) 1760—1766 / *blue*
803	MEISSEN Frederick Augustus III after 1733 / *blue*
804	SELB P. Müller, "Favorit" 1890—1912 / *printed*
805	GRÜNSTADT F. Bartholdi 19th cent. / *blue*
806	WORCESTER Flight, Barr & Barr 1813—1840 / *printed,* *impressed*
807	WORCESTER Flight, Barr & Barr 1813—1840 / *impressed*
808	STADTLENGSFELD Porzellanfabrik A. G. after 1889 / *printed*
809	FULDA Heinrich VIII von Bibra 1770—1788 / *blue*
810	FULDA Adalbert III von Harstall 1788—1789 / *blue*

811 F.F.	**TREVISO** G. & A. Fontebasso c. 1800 / *blue*
812	**SAINT AMAND LES EAUX** J. B. Fauquez 1771—1778 / *blue*
813 F.F. D.	**DALLWITZ** (Dalovice) F. Fischer 1850—1855 / *impressed*
814	**VOLKSTEDT-RUDOLSTADT** F. Greiner 20th cent. / *printed*
815 F K O ⚔ Z	**OBERHOHNDORF** F. Kaestner 1883—20th cent. / *printed*
816	**VALENCIENNES** J. B. Fauquez & Lamoninary 1785—1795 / *blue*
817 FL	**BUDAU** (Budov) F. Lang 1840—1860 / *impressed*
818 *Flight*	**WORCESTER** J. & J. Flight 1783—1792 / *blue*
819 **820** *Flight* *Flight*	**WORCESTER** J. & J. Flight 1783—1792 / *red, blue*
821 *FLIGHTS*	**WORCESTER** J. & J. Flight 1783—1792 / *impressed*
822 *Flight & Barr*	**WORCESTER** J. & J. Flight 1783—1792 / *blue*

823	*Flight*	**WORCESTER** Flight & Barr 1792—1807 / *impressed, printed*
824	*Flight Barr & Barr*	**WORCESTER** Flight, Barr & Barr 1813—1840 / *impressed, printed*
825		**WILHELMSBURG** Aktiengesellschaft after 1882 / *printed*
826		**STOKE-ON-TRENT** Mintons & Hollins 1846—1868 / *printed*
827	F & M	**PIRKENHAMMER** (Březová) Fischer & Mieg 1810—1846 / *impressed*
828	*Fontaine F. 1770*	**LIMOGES** Grellet Frères & Massié 1770—1796 / *blue*
829		**FOËCY** Pillivuyt family after 1800 / *blue*
830		**FOËCY** L. Lourioux 2nd half of 19th cent. / *printed*
831	FOLEY ENGLISH BONE CHINA PAINTED BY HAND 	**FENTON** E. Brain & Co. after 1880 / *printed*

832	ESTABLISHED 18 R & S 50 FOLEY CHINA	FENTON Robinson & Son after 1850 / *printed*
833		FRAUREUTH Porzellanfabrik after 1866 / *printed*
834	F P Nd.Salzbrunn	NIEDER-SALZBRUNN (Szczawienko) F. Prause from 1899 / *blue*
835 836	F.P.C. F.P.C.	ĆMIELÓW K. Cybulski 1870—1884 / *black, impressed*
837	FPM	FREIWALDAU (Gozdnica) H. Schmidt after 1842 / *blue*
838	R	NAPLES Ferdinand IV Rex 1772 / *blue*
839	F&R	PIRKENHAMMER (Březová) Fischer & Reichenbach 1811—1845 / *impressed*
840	FRANCE	FOËCY L. Lourioux 2nd half of 19th cent. / *printed*
841	FRAUREUTH	FRAUREUTH Porzellanfabrik after 1866 / *printed*
842	FU	DALLWITZ (Dalovice) F. Urfus 1855—1875 / *impressed*
843	FURGA	MANTUA, CANETTO SULL'OGLIO Ceramica Furga after 1872 / *printed*

844		**BOW** E. Heylyn & T. Frye 1748—1755 / *blue*
845 **846**		**VERBILKI** F. Gardner after 1767—1800 / *blue*
847		**GERA** J. G. Ehwaldt, J. Gottbrecht and successors 1779—1820 / *blue*
848 **849**		**GOTHA** E. Henneberg 1805—1834 / *blue, various* *colours*
850 **851**		**BERLIN** J. E. Gotzkowsky 1761—1763 / *blue, gold*
852		**GEHREN** J. Günthersfeld & Co. after 1884 / *printed*
853		**DOCCIA** Ginori 1884—1888 / *impressed*
854		**LE NOVE** G. B. Antonibon 1762—1802 / *blue, impressed*
855		**PARIS, RUE DE BONDY** Manufacture du duc d'Angoulême 1781—1793 / *red, gold, blue*

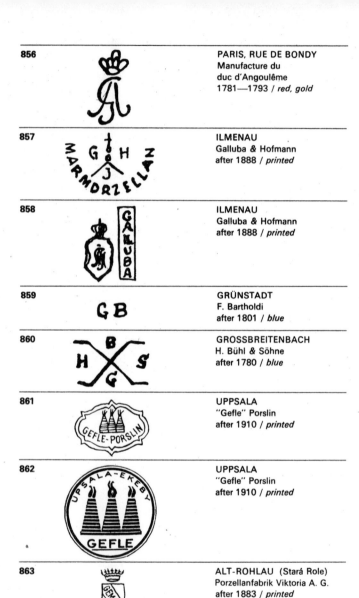

856

PARIS, RUE DE BONDY
Manufacture du
duc d'Angoulême
1781—1793 / *red, gold*

857

ILMENAU
Galluba & Hofmann
after 1888 / *printed*

858

ILMENAU
Galluba & Hofmann
after 1888 / *printed*

859

GRÜNSTADT
F. Bartholdi
after 1801 / *blue*

860

GROSSBREITENBACH
H. Bühl & Söhne
after 1780 / *blue*

861

UPPSALA
"Gefle" Porslin
after 1910 / *printed*

862

UPPSALA
"Gefle" Porslin
after 1910 / *printed*

863

ALT-ROHLAU (Stará Role)
Porzellanfabrik Viktoria A. G.
after 1883 / *printed*

864

GENEVA
J. P. Mühlhauser
1805—1818 / *blue*

865		**GENEVA** J. P. Mühlhauser 1805—1818 / *blue*
866 **867**		**GERONA** "Cordoba" 19th cent. / *blue, red*
868		**OBERKOTZAU** Greiner & Herda after 1893 / *printed*
869		**KATOWICE** Giesche end of 19th cent. / *blue*
870 **871**		**GIESSHÜBEL** (Kysibl) F. Lehnert 1840—1847 / *impressed*
872		**GIESSHÜBEL** (Kysibl) W. von Neuberg 1846—1902 / *impressed*
873	**GI**	**DOCCIA** Ginori 1868—1903 / *blue*
874 **875**	**GIN GINORI**	**DOCCIA** Ginori 1868—1903 / *impressed*
876	*Ginori*	**DOCCIA** Ginori 1884—1901 / *impressed*
877		**MILAN** Richard —Ginori 1903 / *printed*

878		OESLAU W. Goebel after 1879 / *printed*
879		GOTHA August von Gotha *c.* 1805 / *blue*
880		GOTHA E. Henneberg middle of 19th cent. / *blue*
881		GOTHA Morgenroth & Co. after 1866 / *printed*
882		GOTHA E. Pfeffer after 1892 / *blue*
883		UNTERNHAUS Gerarer Porzellanfabrik after 1780 / *blue*
884		GOTHA E. Pfeffer after 1892 / *blue*
885		WORCESTER Grainger & Co. after 1885 / *blue*
886		WORCESTER Grainger, Lee & Co. after 1889 / *blue*
887		GRÄFENTHAL Weiss, Kühnert & Co. after 1891 / *printed*

888		VOLKSTEDT-RUDOLSTADT W. Greiner after 1799 / *impressed, blue*
889		GUSTAVSBERG Ceramic Factory 1845—1880 / *printed*
890		GUSTAVSBERG Ceramic Factory 1866 / *blue*
891		GUSTAVSBERG Ceramic Factory 1910—1940 / *blue*
892		GUSTAVSBERG Ceramic Factory 1930 / *printed*
893 894		GUSTAVSBERG Ceramic Factory 1924 / *printed*
895		GUSTAVSBERG Ceramic Factory 1928 / *printed*
896		GUSTAVSBERG Ceramic Factory 1930 / *printed*
897 898		GUSTAVSBERG Ceramic Factory 1940 / *printed*

899	**GUSTAVSBERG** Ceramic Factory 1943 / *printed*
900	**GEHREN** P. Günthersfeld after 1884 / *printed*
901 902	**STRASBOURG (HAGENAU)** J. A. Hannong after 1768—1784 / *blue*
903 904	**STRASBOURG** P. A. Hannong (Hagenau factory) 1783—1784 / *blue*
905	**PARIS, RUE DE FAUBOURG SAINT DENIS** P. A. Hannong 1771—1776 / *blue*
906	**LOWESTOFT** R. Haward after 1761 / *blue*
907	**MOSCOW** D. Nasonov 1811—1813 / *blue*
908	**LICHTE** Heubach Bros after 1820 / *blue*
909	**MANNHEIM** Rheinische Porzellanfabrik 19th cent. / *impressed*
910 911	**HÜTTENSTEINACH** Schoenau Bros after 1865 / *blue*

912		SCHLAGGENWALD (Slavkov) A. Haas 1847—1867 / printed

912 — *August Haas' in Schlaggenwald*
SCHLAGGENWALD (Slavkov)
A. Haas
1847—1867 / *printed*

913 — *August Haas in Schlaggenwald*
SCHLAGGENWALD (Slavkov)
A. Haas
1847—1867 / *printed*

914 — *August Haas in Schlaggenwald*
SCHLAGGENWALD (Slavkov)
A. Haas
1847—1867 / *printed*

915 — Haas & Czjžek in Schlaggenwald
SCHLAGGENWALD (Slavkov)
Haas & Czjizek
after 1867 / *impressed*

916 — HACKEFORS
HACKEFORS
J. O. Nilson
after 1929 / *printed*

917 — *Hadley* WORCESTER ENGLAND
WORCESTER
Hadley
after 1905 / *printed*

918 — Haidinger
ELBOGEN (Loket)
Haidinger Bros
1833—1873 / *impressed*

919 — Bone China Hammersley & MADE IN ENGLAND
LONGTON
Hammersley & Co.
1860—1870 / *printed*

920 — Robᵗ Havard 1761
LOWESTOFT
R. Haward
after 1761 / *blue*

921		WALDERSHOF J. Haviland 1907—1924 / *printed*
922		KELSTERBACH Ludwig VIII of Hesse-Darmstadt 1767—1768 / *impressed*
923		GROSSBREITENBACH H. Bühl & Söhne after 1780 / *blue, printed*
924		KASSEL Friedrich II of Hesse-Kassel 1766—1788 / *blue*
925		NEUSTADT Heber & Co. after 1900 / *printed*
926		LIMOGES Haviland & Co. after 1797 / *blue*
927		SELB Heinrich & Co. after 1896 / *printed*
928		KELSTERBACH Ludwig VIII of Hesse-Darmstadt 1767—1768 / *blue*
929		KELSTERBACH J. J. Lay 1789—1792 / *incised*
930		KELSTERBACH 1799—1802 / *blue*
931		HELSINKI "Arabia" after 1948 / *printed*

932

HELSINKI
"Arabia"
after 1948 / *printed*

933

HEREND
Porcelain Factory
1855—1898 / *blue*

934

HEREND
Porcelain Factory
1891—1897 / *blue*

935
936

HEREND
Porcelain Factory
1939 / *blue*

937

HEREND
Porcelain Factory
1940 / *blue*

938

HEREND
Porcelain Factory
1899—1939 / *blue*

939

HEREND
Porcelain Factory
1897—1938 / *blue*

940

HEREND
Porcelain Factory
1941 / *blue*

941

HEREND
Porcelain Factory
1855—1898 / *blue*

942	**HEREND** Porcelain Factory 1933—1938 / *blue*
943	**LICHTE** Heubach Bros after 1820 / *blue*
944 945	**STRASBOURG** J. A. Hannong 1768—1781 / *blue*
946	**FENTON** E. Hughes after 1883 / *printed*
947	**BOULOGNE** Haffringue beginning of 19th cent. / *blue*
948	**STRASBOURG** J. A. Hannong 1768—1784 / *blue*
949 950	**HÜTTENSTEINACH** Schoenau Bros after 1865 / *blue*
951	**PIRKENHAMMER** (Březová) Friedrich Höcke 1803—1810 / *blue, gold*
952	**VINCENNES** P. A. Hannong & La Borde 1769—1770 / *blue*
953 954	**VINCENNES** P. A. Hannong & La Borde 1769—1770 / *blue*

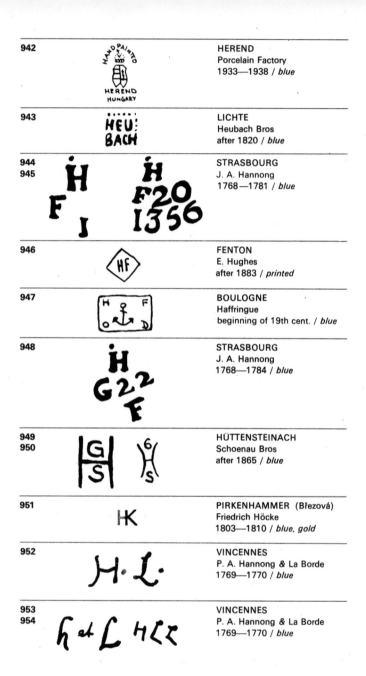

955		LETTIN H. Baensch beginning of 20th cent. *printed*
956		COPENHAGEN J. J. Holm *c.* 1780 / *impressed*
957		LONGTON Hudson & Middleton after 1870 / *printed*
958		COPENHAGEN J. J. Holm *c.* 1780 / *impressed*
959		PROBSTZELLA H. Hutschenreuther after 1886 / *printed*
960		VIERZON Hachez & Pépin *c.* 1879 / *blue*
961		HOHENBERG C. M. Hutschenreuther 1828—1845 / *impressed*
962		HOHENBERG C. M. Hutschenreuther and successors 1890 / *printed*
963		HOHENBERG Hutschenreuther 1914 / *printed*
964		HOHENBERG Hutschenreuther 1914 / *printed*

965 	HOHENBERG Hutschenreuther 1914 / *printed*
966 **967**	LUBENZ (Žlutice) H. Reinl after 1846 / *printed*
968	UNTERWEISSBACH H. Schaubach after 1880 / *printed*
969 	LANE END Hilditsch & Son after 1830 / *blue*
970	SELB L. Hutschenreuther after 1856—1920 / *printed*
971	HÜTTENSTEINACH Schoenau Bros after 1865 / *blue*
972	BOW W. Duesbury 1760—1776 / *blue*
973	ILMENAU C. Nonne c. 1800 / *blue*

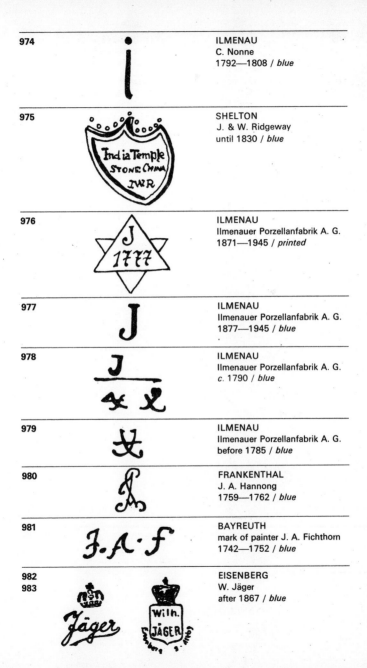

974

ILMENAU
C. Nonne
1792—1808 / *blue*

975

SHELTON
J. & W. Ridgeway
until 1830 / *blue*

India Temple
STONE CHINA
J W R

976

ILMENAU
Ilmenauer Porzellanfabrik A. G.
1871—1945 / *printed*

J
1777

977

ILMENAU
Ilmenauer Porzellanfabrik A. G.
1877—1945 / *blue*

978

ILMENAU
Ilmenauer Porzellanfabrik A. G.
c. 1790 / *blue*

979

ILMENAU
Ilmenauer Porzellanfabrik A. G.
before 1785 / *blue*

980

FRANKENTHAL
J. A. Hannong
1759—1762 / *blue*

981

BAYREUTH
mark of painter J. A. Fichthorn
1742—1752 / *blue*

982
983

EISENBERG
W. Jäger
after 1867 / *blue*

984	**FRIEDLAND** (Frýdlant)
	J. E. Heintschel
	after 1869 / *blue*
985	**VIENNA**
	J. Goldschneider
	after 1882 / *blue*
986	**FRANKENTHAL**
987	J. A. Hannong
	1759—1762 / *blue*
988	**STRASBOURG**
	P. A. Hannong
	1783—1784 / *impressed*
989	**KÖPPELSDORF**
	J. Hering & Sohn
	after 1893 / *printed*
990	**ILMENAU**
	Ilmenauer Porzellanfabrik A. G.
	1871—1945 / *printed*
991	**ILMENAU**
	Ilmenauer Porzellanfabrik A. G.
	1871—1945 / *printed*
992	**VILLEDIEU SUR INDRE**
	J. Lang
	after 1882 / *printed*
993	**PARIS, CLIGNANCOURT**
	J. Moitte
	1789—1798 / *blue*

994	J.P.	**FONTAINEBLEAU** Jacob Petit after 1834 / *blue*
995	J.N.M	**SCHÖNWALD** J. N. Müller after 1879 / *blue*
996	JPF	**ILMENAU** Ilmenauer Porzellanfabrik A. G. 1871—1945 / *printed*
997	J.P L	**LIMOGES** J. Pouyat after 1842 / *blue*
998 **999**	JPM IPM	**ILMENAU** Ilmenauer Porzellanfabrik A. G. 1871—1945 / *printed*
1000 **1001**	"IRIS" JP FinePorcelaine	**KLAUSENBURG (Cluj)** "Iris" Porcelain after 1922 / *printed*
1002	J.S. V.	**VOHENSTRAUSS** J. Seltmann after 1910 / *printed*
1003 **1004**	J. S.	**CHARLOTTENBRUNN** (Zofiówka) J. Schachtel after 1859 / *printed*

1005	ITALY New Stone G. RICHARD & C.	MILAN G. Richard & Co. 1870—1873 / *printed*
1006		KLÖSTERLE (Klášterec) M. Weber 1794—1798 / *blue, red*
1007		KLÖSTERLE (Klášterec) Gräfliche Thun'sche Porzellan-, fabrik 1804—1830 / *blue, gold*
1008		KLÖSTERLE (Klášterec) M. Weber 1794—1798 / *blue*
1009	Korzec	KORZEC M. Mezer after 1803 / *red*
1010		KORZEC M. Mezer after 1803 / *blue, impressed*
1011		LAUF F. Krug after 1871 / *printed*
1012		ELBOGEN (Loket) H. Kretschmann *c.* 1900 / *printed*
1013		OBERHOHNDORF F. Kaestner after 1883 / *printed*

1014	KAHLA Porzellanfabrik after 1844 / *printed*
1015	EISENBERG Porzellanfabrik Kalk G. m. b. H. after 1900 / *printed*
1016	FISCHERN (Rybáře) C. Knoll mid-19th cent. / *printed*
1017	FISCHERN (Rybáře) Karlsbader Porzellanfabrik beginning of 20th cent. *printed*
1018	FISCHERN (Rybáře) Karlsbader Porzellanfabrik 1900—1910 / *printed*
1019	FISCHERN (Rybáře) Karlsbader Porzellanfabrik 1st half of 20th cent. / *printed*
1020	FISCHERN (Rybáře) Karlsbader Porzellanfabrik 1939—1945 / *printed*
1021	FISCHERN (Rybáře) Karlsbader Porzellanfabrik c. 1910 / *printed*

1022	FISCHERN (Rybáře) Karlsbader Porzellanfabrik beginning of 20th cent. *printed*
1023	KARLSKRONA Karlskrona Porslinsfabrik after 1918 / *printed*
1024 	UPPSALA Karlskrona Porslinsfabrik after 1945 / *printed*
1025	KATZHÜTTE J. W. Hamann 19th cent. / *printed*
1026	KATZHÜTTE Hertwig & Co. after 1945 / *printed*
1027	WORCESTER Kerr & Binns 1852—1862 / *printed*
1028	OHRDRUF Kestner 20th cent. / *printed*
1029 	MEISSEN Königliche Hofconditorei Warschau 1713—1806 / *various colours*

1030		LANGEWIESEN O. Schlegelmilch after 1842 / *printed*
1031		COPENHAGEN Bing & Grøndahl after 1905 / *printed*
1032	*Klentsch*	KLENTSCH (Kleneč) A. Schmidt 1835—1889 / *impressed*
1033		WISTRITZ (Bystřice) Krantzberger, Mayer & Purkert after 1911 / *printed*
1034		KÖNIGSZELT (Jaworzyna Śląska) Porcelain Factory after 1860 / *printed*
1035		KÖNIGSZELT (Jaworzyna Śląska) Porcelain Factory after 1860 / *printed*
1036	KODAU	CHODAU (Chodov) J. Hüttner & Co. 1835—1840 / *impressed*
1037		KÖPPELSDORF J. Hering & Sohn after 1893 / *printed*
1038		KORZEC Mérault & Petion 1822 / *red*
1039		KORZEC Mérault & Petion 1830 / *red*

1040	 	KORZEC M. Mezer beginning of 19th cent. / *red*
1041 **1042**		KORZEC M. Mezer beginning of 19th cent. / *red*
1043	 	KORZEC F. Mezer 1793—1814 / *blue*
1044	 	KORZEC F. Mezer 1st half of 19th cent. / *gold*
1045		EISENBERG Porzellanfabrik Kalk G. m. b. H. after 1900 / *printed*
1046	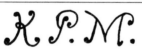	MEISSEN Königl. Porzellanmanufaktur from 1722 / *blue*
1047		MEISSEN Königl. Porzellanmanufaktur 1723—1724 / *blue*
1048	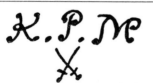	MEISSEN Königl. Porzellanmanufaktur 1723—1724 / *blue*
1049		MEISSEN Königl. Porzellanmanufaktur 1723—1724 / *blue*

1050		BERLIN Königl. Porzellanmanufaktur 1823—1832 / *blue*
1051		WALDENBURG (Walbrzych) Krister Porzellanmanufaktur 1831—1945 / *printed*
1052		WALDENBURG (Walbrzych) Krister Porzellanmanufaktur until 1945 / *printed*
1053		BERLIN Königl. Porzellanmanufaktur 1844—1847 / *blue*
1054		BERLIN Königl. Porzellanmanufaktur from 1857 / *blue*
1055		SCHEIBE-ALSBACH A. W. F. Kister after 1837 / *blue*
1056		SCHEIBE-ALSBACH A. W. F. Kister after 1831 / *blue*
1057		WALDENBURG (Walbrzych) Krister Porzellanmanufaktur after 1900 / *blue*
1058 **1059**		WALDENBURG (Walbrzych) Krister Porzellanmanufaktur after 1831 / *blue*
1060		BERLIN Königl. Porzellanmanufaktur 1837—1844 / *blue*

1061		WALDENBURG (Walbrzych) Krister Porzellanmanufaktur 19th cent. / *blue*
1062		SELB Krautheim & Adelberg after 1884 / *printed*
1063		SELB Krautheim & Adelberg after 1884 / *printed*
1064		WISTRITZ (Bystřice) Krantzberger, Mayer & Purkert after 1911 / *printed*
1065		LANDSTUHL Krister Porzellanmanufaktur after 1952 / *printed*
1066		KRONACH Stockhardt & Schmidt-Eckert after 1912 / *printed*
1067 **1068**		BLANKENHAIN E. Krüger after 1847 / *printed*
1069		TIEFENFURTH (Parowa) K. Steinmann G. m. b. H. 1883—1932 / *printed*

1070	**WALDENBURG** (Walbrzych) Krister Porzellanmanufaktur 19th cent. / *blue*
1071	**LUDWIGSBURG** Ludwig Eugen of Württemberg 1793—1795 / *blue*
1072 **1073** **1074**	**LILLE** Leperre-Durot 1784—1817 / *blue*
1075	**ORLÉANS** Benoist Le Brun 1806—1812 / *red*
1076 **1077**	**SCHORNDORF** Bauer & Pfeiffer 1904—1939 / *printed*
1078	**PARIS, GROS CAILLOU** J. Jacquemart (L. Broillet) 1765—1773 / *blue*
1079	**VALENCIENNES** J. B. Fauquez & Lamoninary 1785—1795 / *blue*
1080 **1081** **1082**	**PARIS, RUE DE REUILLY** J. J. Lassia 1774—1784 / *red, gold*
1083	**PASSAU** Lenck family 2nd half of 19th cent. / *printed*
1084	**LIMBACH** G. Greiner 1772—1787 / *blue*
1085	**VALENCIENNES** J. B. Fauquez & Lamoninary 1785—1795 / *blue*

1086 **1087**		LETTIN H. Baensch 1858—1945 / *printed*
1088		LUDWIGSBURG Ludwig Eugen of Württemberg 1793—1795 / *blue*
1089		LANGEWIESEN O. Schlegelmilch after 1892 / *printed*
1090		LISBON J. J. Paszoa after 1870 / *printed*
1091		KRUMMENNAAB H. Lange & Co. after 1934 / *printed*
1092 **1093**		LUXEMBOURG Bloch Sept Fontaines 19th cent. / *blue*
1094 **1095**		LUXEMBOURG Bloch Sept Fontaines 19th cent. / *blue*
1096		LASSAY Comte de Lauraguais-Brancas 1763—1768 / *blue, various colours*
1097		LUXEMBOURG Bloch Sept Fontaines 19th cent. / *blue, various colours*
1098		LUXEMBOURG Bloch Sept Fontaines 19th cent. / *blue*

1099	LUXEMBOURG Bloch Sept Fontaines 19th cent. / *impressed*
1100 **1101**	LASSAY Comte de Lauraguais-Brancas 1763—1768 / *incised*
1102	LIMBACH G. Greiner 1762—1787 / *incised*
1103	LIMBACH G. Greiner 1762—1787 / *blue*
1104	ORLÉANS Benoist Le Brun 1806—1812 / *blue*
1105 **1106**	BRUSSELS L. Cretté 1791—1803 / *blue*
1107	BRUSSELS L. Cretté 1791—1803 / *blue*
1108	BRUSSELS L. Cretté 1791—1803 / *blue*
1109	BRUSSELS L. Cretté 1791—1803 / *blue*
1110	DERBY Royal Crown Porcelain Co. from 1876 / *printed*

1111		**LETTIN** H. Baensch after 1858 / *blue*
1112		**LETTIN** Porzellanfabrik after 1945 / *printed*
1113 **1114**		**LETTIN** H. Baensch after 1858 / *blue*
1115		**KAHLA** C. A. Lehmann & Sohn after 1895 / *printed*
1116		**LICHTE** Heubach Bros after 1820 / *blue*
1117		**SCHLAGGENWALD** (Slavkov) J. Lippert & A. Haas 1830—1846 / *impressed*
1118		**SELB** L. Hutschenreuther after 1920—1938 / *printed*
1119		**ALT-ROHLAU** (Stará Role) J. Schneider & Co. after 1904 / *blue*

1120	*a Lille*	**LILLE** Leperre-Durot 1784—1817 / *blue, red, gold*
1121		**LIMBACH** Greiner family 1882 / *printed*
1122 **1123**		**LIMBACH** Greiner family 1882 / *printed*
1124		**LIMOGES** Royal Porcelain Factory J. F. Alluaud 1788—1793 / *blue*
1125		**LIMOGES** Royal Porcelain Factory 1784—1796 / *blue, red, gold*
1126	J.P L	**LIMOGES** J. Pouyat after 1842 / *green*
1127	X	**LIMBACH** G. Greiner 1772—1787 / *blue*
1128	X *	**LIMBACH** G. Greiner 1772—1787 / *blue*

1129	*porcelaine royalle de Limoges* C D	LIMOGES Royal Porcelain Factory Comte d'Artois 1771—1784 / *blue, red, gold, incised*
1130	LIMOGES B & Cie FRANCE	LIMOGES H. A. Balleroy Frères 19th cent. / *blue*
1131	LIMOGES J·B & Cie FRANCE	LIMOGES J. Balleroy & Co. 19th cent. / *blue*
1132	B & Co LIMOGES (FRANCE)	LIMOGES L. Bernardaux & Co. after 1863 / *blue*
1133	B & Co LIMOGES FRANCE	LIMOGES L. Bernardaux & Co. after 1863 / *printed*
1134	LIMOGES BRP FRANCE	LIMOGES Beulé, Reboisson & Parot 19th cent. / *blue, printed*
1135	PORCELAINE ARTISTIQUE DE LIMOGES BARBOTINE F. M. GRAND FEU	LIMOGES Fontanille & Marraud after 1925 / *printed*
1136	PORCELAINE ARTISTIQUE F. M. LIMOGES FRANCE MADE IN F² LIMOGES M FRANCE	LIMOGES Fontanille & Marraud 19th cent. / *printed*
1137	FRANCE M DE M LIMOGES	LIMOGES Granger & Co. 19th cent. / *printed*

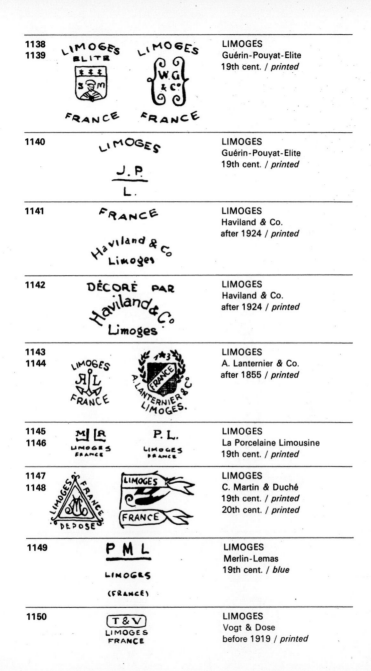

1138 **1139**	LIMOGES Guérin-Pouyat-Elite 19th cent. / *printed*
1140	LIMOGES Guérin-Pouyat-Elite 19th cent. / *printed*
1141	LIMOGES Haviland & Co. after 1924 / *printed*
1142	LIMOGES Haviland & Co. after 1924 / *printed*
1143 **1144**	LIMOGES A. Lanternier & Co. after 1855 / *printed*
1145 **1146**	LIMOGES La Porcelaine Limousine 19th cent. / *printed*
1147 **1148**	LIMOGES C. Martin & Duché 19th cent. / *printed* 20th cent. / *printed*
1149	LIMOGES Merlin-Lemas 19th cent. / *blue*
1150	LIMOGES Vogt & Dose before 1919 / *printed*

1151	R&Cº LIMOGES FRANCE	LIMOGES Raynaud & Co. 1919 / *printed*
1152		LIMOGES Raynaud & Co. after 1919 / *printed*
1153		LIMOGES Rousset & Guillerot 20th cent. / *printed*
1154	 ANCIENNE FABRIQUE ROYALE LIMOGES·FRANCE	LIMOGES Societé Porcelainière de Limoges 20th cent. / *printed*
1155		LIMOGES Fabrique de Porcelaines Blanches & Décorées Anciens Ets. after 1908 / *printed*
1156	T.L.B LIMOGES	LIMOGES Touze, Lemaître Frères & Blancher 19th cent. / *printed*
1157 1158	UC Limoges FRANCE / Limoges UC FRANCE	LIMOGES Union Céramique 19th cent. / *printed*
1159 1160	U L LIMOGES FRANCE / LIMOGES ULIM FRANCE	LIMOGES Union Limousine after 1908 / *printed*
1161	A.VIGNAUD FRANCE LIMOGES	LIMOGES A. Vignaud after 1911 / *printed*

1162	LIMOGES Villegoureix 19th cent. / *printed*
1163	LIMOGES A. Vignaud after 1911 / *blue*
1164	LIMOGES Villegoureix 19th cent. / *printed*
1165	SCHLAGGENWALD (Slavkov) J. Lippert & A. Haas 1830—1846 / *impressed*
1166	SCHLAGGENWALD (Slavkov) J. Lippert & A. Haas 1830—1846 / *printed*
1167	LISBON J. M. Perreira end of 18th cent. / *gold, red*
1168	LIMOGES Manuf. de Porcelaines Ets. Legrand 19th cent. / *printed*
1169	LIMBACH G. Greiner 1772—1787 / *blue*
1170 1171	VINCENNES Royal Porcelain Factory 1740—1752 / *blue*
1172	VINCENNES Royal Porcelain Factory 1740—1752 / *blue*

1173		VINCENNES Royal Porcelain Factory 1740—1752 / *blue*
1174		VINCENNES Royal Porcelain Factory 1740—1752 / *gold*
1175		VINCENNES Royal Porcelain Factory 1753—1756 / *blue*
1176		VINCENNES Royal Porcelain Factory 1754 / *blue*
1177		VINCENNES Royal Porcelain Factory 1755 / *blue*
1178		VINCENNES Royal Porcelain Factory 1740—1752 / *blue*
1179		VINCENNES Royal Porcelain Factory 1753—1756 / *blue*
1180		SÈVRES Royal Porcelain Factory 1778 / *blue, various colours*
1181		SÈVRES Royal Porcelain Factory (hard-paste) 1756 / *blue, various colours*

1182		SÈVRES Royal Porcelain Factory (hard-paste) 1769—1793 / *blue, various* *colours*
1183		COALPORT imitation of Sèvres mark 1860—1880 / *blue*
1184		FOËCY L. Lourioux 19th cent. / *printed*
1185		FENTON E. Hughes after 1883 / *printed*
1186		LONGTON Hammersley & Co. *c.* 1900 / *printed*
1187	A Trefle From LOWESTOFT	LOWESTOFT R. Allen after 1802 / *blue*
1188	James & Mary Curtis Lowestoft	LOWESTOFT James & Mary Curtis after 1757—1771 / *black*
1189		VINCENNES Louis Philippe, duc de Chartres 1777—1788 / *blue*
1190		PARIS, RUE AMELOT under the aegis of Louis Philippe, duc d'Orléans 1786—1793 / *blue*

1191		ORLÉANS Benoist Le Brun 1806—1812 / *red*
1192		VINCENNES Louis Philippe, duc de Chartres 1777—1788 / *blue*
1193		BORDEAUX Lahens & Rateau after 1819 / *blue*
1194		LA SEYNIE Marquis de Beaupoil & Co. 1774—1789 / *blue, red*
1195		LA SEYNIE E. Baignol 1789—1856 / *blue, red*
1196		LA SEYNIE E. Baignol 1789—1856 / *blue, red*
1197		VENDRENNES M. Lozelet after 1800 / *blue*
1198		LUBARTÓW Count H. Lubieński 1840—1850 / *impressed*
1199		LUBARTÓW Count H. Lubieński 1840—1850 / *impressed*
1200		LUBARTÓW Count H. Lubieński 1840—1850 / *impressed*
1201		PODERSAM (Podbořany) Porzellanfabrik "Alp" G. m. b. H. 1920—1941 / *printed*

1202	SCHORNDORF Bauer & Pfeiffer 1904—1939 / *printed*
1203	VINOVO G. Lormello 1815—1820 / *blue*
1204	VALENCIENNES Lamoninary 1800—1810 / *blue, red, brown,* *black*
1205	VALENCIENNES Lamoninary 1800—1810 / *blue, red, brown,* *black*
1206	SCHORNDORF Bauer & Pfeiffer 1904—1939 / *printed*
1207	SCHORNDORF Bauer & Pfeiffer 1904—1939 / *printed*
1208	FLORENCE Francesco II Medici 1578—1587 / *blue*
1209	VOLKSTEDT-RUDOLSTADT G. H. Macheleid 1760—1762 / *violet*
1210	PARIS, CLIGNANCOURT Fabrique de Monsieur 1775—1793 / *red*

1211 1212		PARIS, CLIGNANCOURT J. Moitte 1793—1798 / *blue*
1213		SCHWARZA-SAALBAHN E. & A. Müller after 1890 / *blue*
1214 1215		STOKE-ON-TRENT T. Minton 1793—1835 / *various colours, gold*
1216		HANLEY Booths & Colclough Ltd. 20th cent. / *printed*
1217	M A	CHANTILLY M. Aron Père after 1845 / *printed*
1218		MAYERHÖFEN Benedikt Bros 1883—1918 / *printed*
1219		MÄBENDORF Mathes & Ebel after 1882 / *printed*
1220 1221		MÄBENDORF Mathes & Ebel after 1882 / *printed*
1222 1223		MARIEBERG P. Berthevin 1766—1769 / *incised*
1224		MARIEBERG P. Berthevin 1766—1769 / *incised*

1225		MARIEBERG H. Sten and J. Dortu 1777—1778 / *blue*
1226		ELGERSBURG E. & F. C. Arnoldi after 1808 / *blue*
1227		HOHENBERG C. M. Hutschenreuther 1860 / *impressed*
1228 1229		LA MONCLOA Royal Porcelain Factory 1817—1850 / *red*
1230		MEHUN-SUR-YÈVRE Pillivuyt & Co. after 1853 / *blue*
1231		EICHWALD (Dubí) Dr Widera & Co.; imitation of Meissen with onion pattern 19th—20th cent. / *blue*
1232		KÖNITZ Metzel Bros after 1909 / *blue*
1233		LUBAU (Hlubany) Martin Bros after 1874 / *blue*
1234		KÖNITZ Metzel Bros 1909—1950 / *blue*
1235		KÖNITZ Metzel Bros 1909—1950 / *blue*

1236		**MILAN** S. Richard after 1883 / *blue*
1237		**DELFT** Ary de Milde end of 17th cent. / *impressed*
1238 **1239**		**STOKE-ON-TRENT** T. Minton and successors 1941 / *printed*
1240		**HANLEY** "Blue Mist" 20th cent. / *printed*
1241 **1242**		**MITTERTEICH** Porzellanfabrik after 1917 / *printed*
1243		**MITTERTEICH** Porzellanfabrik after 1917 / *printed*
1244		**SÈVRES** period of the Consulate 1803—1804 / *red, printed*

1245		ILMENAU Metzler Bros & Ortloff after 1875 / *blue*
1246		PARIS, RUE AMELOT Manufacture du duc d'Orléans (J. B. Outrequin) 1786—1793 / *red, gold*
1247		MOABIT M. Schuman & Sohn 1835 / *blue*
1248	M:OL.	OUDE LOOSDRECHT J. de Mol 1771—1784 / *incised*
1249	M:OL.	OUDE LOOSDRECHT J. de Mol 1771—1784 / *black, various colours*
1250	M:oL	OUDE LOOSDRECHT J. de Mol 1771—1784 / *red, various colours*
1251	M.O.L *	OUDE LOOSDRECHT Manufacture Oude Loosdrecht after 1784 / *blue, gold*
1252	M:OL.	OUDE LOOSDRECHT J. de Mol 1771—1784 / *impressed*
1253	MoL Lm3	OUDE LOOSDRECHT J. de Mol 1771—1784 / *violet*
1254	M.ol N°10	OUDE LOOSDRECHT J. de Mol 1771—1784 / *blue, impressed*
1255	M:oL	OUDE LOOSDRECHT J. de Mol 1771—1784 / *impressed*

1256	M:oL A	OUDE LOOSDRECHT J. de Mol 1771—1784 / *blue*
1257	M·OL L 27	OUDE LOOSDRECHT J. de Mol 1771—1784 / *gold, violet*
1258	M: o:L 87	OUDE LOOSDRECHT Manufacture Oude Loosdrecht after 1784 / *blue*
1259	M0 Moitte	PARIS, CLIGNANCOURT J. Moitte 1793—1798 / *blue*
1260 1261	M X O I	ILMENAU Metzler Bros & Ortloff after 1875 / *printed*
1262	MONCLOA	LA MONCLOA Royal Porcelain Factory 1817—1850 / *impressed*
1263	MOSA MAASTRICHT (FABRIEKSMERK)	MAASTRICHT L. Regout & Zonen after 1883 / *printed*
1264	RM Moschendorf BAVARIA	HOF-MOSCHENDORF O. Reinecke after 1878 / *printed*
1265 1266	MP· AP	ETIOLLES J. B. Monier & D. Pellevé 1768—1770 / *incised*
1267	M.P.M.	MEISSEN Meissener Porzellanmanufaktur after 1722 / *blue*

1268

MAASTRICHT
Manufaktur Porselein Mosa
after 1883 / *printed*

1269

BAYREUTH
S. P. Meyer
after 1900 / *printed*

1270

VOLKSTEDT-RUDOLSTADT
Müller & Co.
after 1907 / *printed*

1271

VOLOKITINO
A. Miklaszewski
1820—1864 / *printed*

1272
1273

NAPLES
Royal Porcelain Factory
1771—1834 / *blue, impressed*

1274
1275

NAPLES
Royal Porcelain Factory
1771—1834 / *blue, impressed*

1276

NAPLES
Royal Porcelain Factory
1771—1834 / *blue*

1277

SÈVRES
2nd Empire period
1852—1870 / *red*

1278

DOCCIA
casts of Capodimonte models
1850—1903 / *blue*

1279 1280		LE NOVE Antonibon family end of 18th—19th cent. *incised*
1281		NIDERVILLER A. P. de Custine—C. F. Lanfrey 1780—1800 / *black*
1282		SHELTON, NEW HALL New Hall China Factory 1781—1825 / *blue*
1283 1284	N ▮	ALT-HALDENSLEBEN Nathusius after 1826 / *blue*
1285	👑 N	VOLKSTEDT-RUDOLSTADT E. Bohne & Söhne 1854—1900 / *blue*
1286		VOLKSTEDT-RUDOLSTADT K. Ens after 1898 / *blue*
1287	*N* = 3 6 = w	MEISSEN Königliche Porzellanmanufaktur numbered white porcelain to no. 68 before 1725 / *blue*
1288	*N* 198 ✳ TTL	CHELSEA 19th cent. / *impressed*
1289	*Nantgar.v*	NANTGARW W. Billingsley & S. Walker 1813—1822 / *blue*
1290	NANTGARW.	NANTGARW W. Billingsley & S. Walker 1813—1822 / *impressed*

1291	NAST.	PARIS, RUE POPINCOURT J. N. H. Nast 1782—1835 / *red, gold*
1292	NAST a PARIS	PARIS, RUE POPINCOURT J. N. H. Nast 1782—1835 / *red, gold*
1293		COALPORT Coalport, Nantgarw, Swansea 1861 / *gold*
1294	*New Hall*	SHELTON, NEW HALL Hollins & Warburton *c.* 1800 / *printed*
1295		VOLKSTEDT-RUDOLSTADT K. Ens after 1898 / *blue*
1296		LUNÉVILLE P. L. Cyfflé 1769—1780 / *blue*
1297 1298	N.G. N.G.F.	GIESSHÜBEL (Kysibl) W. von Neuberg 1847—1902 / *impressed*
1299	*Nider*	NIDERVILLER A. P. de Custine—C. F. Lanfrey 1780—1800 / *black*
1300	NIDERVILLER	NIDERVILLER A. P. de Custine—C. F. Lanfrey end of 18th cent. / *impressed*
1301	*Niderviller*	NIDERVILLER A. P. de Custine—C. F. Lanfrey 1780—1800 / *black*

1302	Nove ✳	LE NOVE Antonibon family from 1781 / *gold*
1303	ƎΛOΝ Nove	LE NOVE Antonibon family 1763—1773 / *relief*
1304	·Nove	LE NOVE Antonibon family from 1781 / *incised*
1305	G.B. NOVE	LE NOVE G. Baroni 1802—1825 / *various colours*
1306	NOVE ✳	LE NOVE G. Baroni 1802—1825 / *impressed*
1307	ue No:☙ G·B·A·B:	LE NOVE G. B. Antonibon from 1762 / *gold, various colours*
1308	Houe. AntonioBon	LE NOVE Antonibon family 1762—1802 / *red*
1309	Fabbrica Baroni Nove.	LE NOVE G. Baroni 1802—1825 / *blue*

1310	G B NOVE	LE NOVE G. Baroni 1802—1825 / *blue*
1311	F. P. M. O. D. NOVI SAD	NOVI SAD Fabrika porculana after 1922 / *printed*
1312	NOWOTNY ALTROHLAU	ALT-ROHLAU (Stará Role) A. Nowotny 1838—1884 / *impressed*
1313	N&R	ILMENAU C. Nonne & K. Roesch 1808—1871 / *printed*
1314	.N.S.	OTTWEILER Prince of Nassau-Saarbrücken 1763—1794 / *blue, gold*
1315	n·s W·1766	OTTWEILER Prince of Nassau-Saarbrücken (manager H. Wagner) 1766 / *incised*
1316	O & E.G. ROYAL AUSTRIA	ALT-ROHLAU (Stará Role) O. & E. Gutherz 1899—1918 / *printed*
1317	B & P O	OHRDRUF Baehr & Proeschild after 1871 / *printed*
1318	OISSEL B.P.&C. NORMANDE LACÉRAMIQUE	OISSEL La Céramique "Normande" 20th cent. / *printed*

1319		ORLÉANS
		G. d'Aureaubert
		1753—1783 / *blue*

1320		BOURG LA REINE
		J. Jullien & S. Jacques
		1773—1804 / *printed*

1321		TRIPTIS
		Triptis A. G. Porzellanfabrik
		after 1891 / *printed*

1322		TRIPTIS
		Triptis A. G. Porzellanfabrik
		after 1891 / *printed*

1323		PRAGUE
1324		K. Kriegel & Co.
		after 1837 / *impressed*

1325		KORZEC
		Merault & Petion
		1815—1929 / *blue*

1326		KORZEC
		Petion
		1815—1829 / *blue, red, gold, impressed*

1327		LORIENT
		Charey, Sauvageau & Hervé
		c. 1800 / *blue*

1328		PINXTON
1329		W. Billingsley & J. Coke
		1796—1813 / *red*

1330		ETIOLLES
		D. Pellevé
		1768—1770 / *incised*

1331		SCHMIEDEBERG (Kowary)
		Pohl Bros
		after 1871 / *blue*

1332		PROBSTZELLA H. Hutschenreuther after 1886 / *printed*
1333		HELSINKI "Arabia" after 1948 / *printed*
1334		ILMENAU A. Fischer after 1907 / *printed*
1335	*Palme*	SCHELTEN (Šelty) J. Palme after 1829 / *impressed*
1336	PALME	SCHELTEN (Šelty) J. Palme after 1829 / *printed*
1337	S: L: PALME IN SCHELTEN BEI HAYDA	SCHELTEN (Šelty) J. Palme 1851—1860 / *printed*
1338	PARAGON BY APPOINTMENT FINE BONE CHINA ENGLAND REG?	LONGTON Paragon China Ltd after 1919 / *printed*
1339	P C G MANUFACTURE du petit Carousel Paris	PARIS, RUE DU PETIT CARROUSEL C. B. Guy 1789—1800 / *red, gold*
1340	G. h Rue Thirou a Paris	PARIS, RUE THIROUX Housel & Guy 1797—1798 / *red*

1341	MANUFRE de MGR le Duc d'angouleme a Paris	PARIS, RUE DE BONDY Manufacture du duc d'Angoulême 1781—1793 / *red*
1342	MANUFRe de MM Guerhard et Dihla Paris	PARIS, RUE DE BONDY J. Dihl & Guerhard 1793—1817 / *red*
1343	MANUFRE DE PORCELAINE DU Cen NAST A PARIS	PARIS, RUE POPINCOURT J. N. H. Nast 1782—1835 / *incised*
1344	**PB**	PARIS, RUE DE CRUSSOL C. Potter & Blancheron 1792—beginning of 19th cent. *blue*
1345	PB	IRÚN Luso Espanola de Porcelanas, Fabrica de Bidosa after 1935 / *printed*
1346	CPC	CREIDLITZ Porzellanfabrik A. G. after 1907 / *printed*
1347	c P G	PARIS, RUE DU PETIT CARROUSEL C. B. Guy 1789—1800 / *red, gold*
1348	TP	GOTHA E. Pfeffer after 1892 / *printed*
1349	P PG	GEHREN Porzellanfabrik Günthersfeld A. G. after 1884 / *printed*
1350	PH	STRASBOURG Paul A. Hannong 1751—1754 / *incised, blue*

1351	STRASBOURG Paul A. Hannong 1751—1754 / *impressed*
PH	
1352	STRASBOURG (HAGENAU) Pierre A. Hannong (Hagenau factory) 1783—1784 / *blue*
1353	STRASBOURG (HAGENAU) Pierre A. Hannong (Hagenau factory) 1783—1784 / *incised*
1354 **1355** PHF PH F	FRANKENTHAL Paul A. Hannong 1755—1759 / *impressed*
1356 PICKMAN Y.GA. CHINA OPACA SEVILLA	SEVILLE "La Cartuja"; de Aponte, Pickmann & Co. after 1867 / *printed*
1357 PICKMANN Y C CHINA OPACA	SEVILLE "La Cartuja"; de Aponte, Pickmann & Co. after 1867 / *printed*
1358 P&F France	FOËCY C. H. Pillivuyt 2nd half of 19th cent. / *printed*
C. H. PILLIVUYT & Cie Paris. PARIS. FOESCY. MEHUN.	
1359 PILIVITE PORCELAINES A FEU PILLIVUYT&Cⁱᵉ MEHUN FRANCE	MEHUN-SUR-YÈVRE C. H. Pillivuyt after 1852 / *printed*
1360 PINK Vogue BONE CHINA MADE IN ENGLAND	HANLEY Booths & Colclough Ltd 19th cent. / *printed*

1361		**PIRKENHAMMER** (Březová) "Epiag" 1918—1938 / *printed*
1362	P R	**KORZEC** Petion 1815—1828 / *red*
1363		**PARIS, RUE AMELOT** Manufacture du duc d'Orléans 1786—1793 / *blue*
1364	PK BAVARIA	**KRUMMENNAAB** Illinger & Co. after 1931 / *printed*
1365	Made Cecho PKD SlovaKia	**KALTENHOF** (Oblanov) J. Dietel 1918—1938 / *printed*
1366	P L	**STADTLENGSFELD** Porzellanfabrik A. G. after 1889 / *printed*
1367	Planken Hammer Floss Gbrf.	**PLANKENHAMMER** Fross Bros after 1908 / *printed*
1368	PLANT TUSCAN CHINA MADE IN ENGLAND	**LONGTON** R. H. Plant & Co. after 1880 / *printed*
1369	PL S	**SCHLACKENWERTH** (Ostrov) Pfeiffer & Löwenstein 20th cent. / *printed*
1370	PLS	**SCHLACKENWERTH** (Ostrov) Pfeiffer & Löwenstein 20th cent. / *printed*

1371		**HOF MOSCHENDORF** O. Reinecke after 1878 / *printed*
1372		**POSCHETZAU (Božičany)** Maier & Co. 1938—1945 / *printed*
1373		**OBERKOTZAU** Neuerer K. G. after 1943 / *printed*
1374		**PONTENX** De Rosly 1779—1790 / *blue*
1375		**POTSCHAPPEL** C. Thieme after 1872 / *printed*
1376		**POTSCHAPPEL** C. Thieme after 1872 / *printed*
1377	**Potter** **Paris** **86**	**PARIS, RUE DE CRUSSOL** Manufacture du prince de Galles (C. Potter) 1789—1792 / *blue*
1378		**FREIWALDAU (Gozdnica)** H. Schmidt 20th cent. / *printed*

1379	**PLANKENHAMMER** Porzellanfabrik after 1908 / *printed*
1380 **1381** PRAG K&C PRAG	**PRAGUE** K. Kriegel & Co. after 1837 / *impressed*
1382 Prag	**PRAGUE** K. Kriegel & Co. after 1837 / *impressed*
1383 P & S	**CHODAU** (Chodov) Portheim & Sohn *c.* 1870 / *impressed*
1384	**POTSCHAPPEL** C. Thieme after 1872 / *blue*
1385 P S	**SORAU** (Żary) C. & E. Carstens after 1918 / *printed*
1386	**STADTLENGSFELD** Porzellanfabrik A. G. after 1889 / *printed*
1387	**SCHLACKENWERTH** (Ostrov) Pfeiffer & Löwenstein 1st half of 20th cent. / *printed*
1388 PR	**FRANKENTHAL** P. van Recum 1795 / *blue*
1389 P.Y.C 72	**SEVILLE** "La Cartuja"; de Aponte, Pickmann & Co. after 1867 / *printed*

1390	ZWEIBRÜCKEN, GUTENBRUNN
	Christian IV of Pfalz-Zweibrücken
	1768—1775 / *blue*

1391	LONGTON
	Shore & Coggins Ltd
	19th cent. / *printed*

1392	ALT-ROHLAU (Stará Role)
	A. Nowotny
	1838—1884 / *impressed*

1393	LUDWIGSBURG
1394	Fridericus Rex
	1806—1816 / *red, gold*

1395	FRANKENTHAL
	P. van Recum
	1797—1799 / *blue*

1396	RAUENSTEIN
	Greiner Bros
	after 1783 / *blue*

1397	VOLKSTEDT-RUDOLSTADT
	Holzapfel & Greiner
	1799—1817 / *blue*

1398	VOLKSTEDT-RUDOLSTADT
	Holzapfel & Greiner
	1799—1817 / *blue*

1399	GOTHA
	W. von Rothberg
	1757—1783 / *blue*

1400	GOTHA
	C. Schultz, Gabel & Brehm
	1783—1805 / *blue*

1401 **1402**		MARSEILLE J. G. Robert 1773—1793 / *blue, black,* *red, gold*
1403		RÖRSTRAND Porcelain Factory 20th cent. / *blue*
1404		MILAN G. Richard 1842—1860 / *blue*
1405		MILAN G. Richard *c.* 1850 / *blue*
1406		MILAN G. Richard 1870 / *blue*
1407		MILAN G. Richard 1860—1870 / *blue*
1408		MILAN G. Richard *c.* 1870 / *blue*
1409 **1410**		SAINT UZE G. Revol Père & Fils after 1780 / *blue*
1411		MITTERTEICH J. Rieber after 1868 / *printed*

1412	**MITTERTEICH** J. Rieber after 1868 / *printed* R with crown CAMBRIDGE *Ivory*
1413	**ROSCHÜTZ** Unger & Schilde 1821 / *printed*
1414	**ROSCHÜTZ** Unger & Schilde and successors 20th cent. / *printed*
1415	**SCHMIEDEBERG (Kowary)** Pohl Bros after 1871 / *printed*
1416	**FENTON** S. Radford Ltd after 1883 / *printed* RADFORDS BONE CHINA FENTON STOKE-ON-TRENT
1417	**FENTON** S. Radford Ltd after 1883 / *printed* RADFORDS CROWN CHINA MADE IN ENGLAND
1418	**LONGTON** Hall Bros Ltd after 1947 / *printed* HB RADNOR BONE CHINA ENGLAND
1419	**SELB** Rosenthal A. G. 1891—1907 / *printed*

1420	**STOKE-ON-TRENT** Mintons & Hollins 1867 / *printed*
1421	**TURIN** G. G. Rosetti after 1742 / *blue*
1422 **1423**	**SÈVRES** First Republic period 1793—1800 / *blue*
1424	**FRANKENTHAL** J. N. van Recum 1797—1799 / *blue*
1425	**CHODAU (Chodov)** Richter, Falke & Hahn after 1882 / *printed*
1426	**CHODAU (Chodov)** Richter, Falke & Hahn 1918—1945 / *printed*
1427	**CHODAU (Chodov)** Richter, Falke & Hahn 1918—1945 / *printed*
1428	**LA MONCLOA** Ferdinand VII of Spain 1817—1850 / *blue*
1429	**EISENBERG** F. A. Reinecke after 1796 / *blue*

1430	$\mathcal{R}$-g	GOTHA C. Schultz & Co. 1783—1805 / *blue*
1431	*G. R.*	MILAN G. Richard 1860 / *blue*
1432 1433	G. R R.	MILAN G. Richard 1842 / *blue*
1434		DOCCIA G. Richard after 1896 / *printed*
1435	*R.n*	RAUENSTEIN Greiner Bros 1783—19th cent. / *blue, impressed*
1436	G. RICHARD SON BARONA	MILAN G. Richard 1847 / *printed*
1437	JULIUS RICHARD & C S. CRISTOFORO	MILAN G. Richard 1850—1860 / *printed*
1438		MILAN G. Richard 1885 / *printed*
1439	G. Richard	MILAN G. Richard 1868—1881 / *printed*
1440		MILAN G. Richard 1883 / *printed*

1441 	SHELTON J. & W. Ridgeway after 1853 / *printed*
1442	GRÜNLAS R. Kampf after 1911 / *printed*
1443	SELB L. Hutschenreuther after 1856 / *printed*
1444	RAUENSTEIN Greiner Bros 1800—1850 / *blue*
1445	RAUENSTEIN Greiner Bros after 1850 / *blue*
1446 	ALT-ROHLAU (Stará Role) A. Nowotny 1838—1884 / *printed*
1447	ALT-ROHLAU (Stará Role) A. Nowotny 1838—1884 / *impressed*
1448 	COALPORT J. Rose & Co. c. 1850 / *printed*
1449	SELB Rosenthal A. G. after 1908 / *printed*
1450	KRONACH Rosenthal & Co. 1933—1953 / *printed*

1451 	**SELB** Rosenthal A. G. after 1867 / *printed*
1452	**ROSSLAU** H. Schomburg & Söhne 19th cent. / *printed*
1453	**RÖRSTRAND** Duke Charles after 1809 / *blue*
1454	**RÖRSTRAND** Porcelain Factory 1838—1840 / *impressed*
1455 	**RÖRSTRAND** Porcelain Factory mid-19th cent. / *printed*
1456 	**RÖRSTRAND** Porcelain Factory 1852 / *blue, gold*
1457 	**RÖRSTRAND** Porcelain Factory 1857—1860 / *brown*
1458	**RÖRSTRAND** Porcelain Factory from 1870 / *various colours*

1459

GRÜNLAS
R. Kampf
from 1911 / *printed*

1460

MANNHEIM
Rheinische Porzellanfabrik
after 1910 / *printed*

1461
1462

SUHL
E. Schlegelmilch
after 1861 / *printed*

1463
1464

TILLOWITZ (Tulowice)
R. Schlegelmilch
after 1869 / *printed*

1465

FENTON
S. Radford Ltd
after 1883 / *printed*

1466

TURIN
G. G. Rosetti
mid-18th cent. / *blue*

1467

SCHORNDORF
C. M. Bauer & Pfeiffer
1904 / *printed*

1468

ROYAL-STONE
G. RICHARD & C.

MILAN
G. Richard
1870—1873 / *printed*

1469	**ROZENBURG** Porcelain Factory 1885—1905 / *printed*
1470 **1471**	**SCHLAGGENWALD (Slavkov)** J. J. Paulus — L. Greiner 1793—1812 / *blue*
1472	**SCHLAGGENWALD (Slavkov)** J. J. Lippert & V. Haas 1810—1820 / *gold*
1473	**SCHLAGGENWALD (Slavkov)** J. J. Lippert & V. Haas 1810—1820 / *blue*
1474	**SCHLAGGENWALD (Slavkov)** J. J. Lippert & V. Haas 1810—1820 / *impressed*
1475 **1476**	**PARIS, RUE DE LA ROQUETTE** Souroux after 1773 / *blue, red*
1477	**CAUGHLEY** T. Turner after 1783 / *blue*
1478 **1479**	**SCHNEY** E. Liebmann after 1800 / *blue*
1480	**SCHEIBE-ALSBACH** A. W. F. Kister after 1834 / *blue*
1481	**SAINT VALLIER** M. Montagne after 1830 / *printed*

1482	**GOTHA** Simson Bros after 1883 / *printed*
1483	**KÖPPELSDORF-NORD** Swaine & Co. after 1854 / *printed*
1484	**SITZENDORF** Voigt Bros after 1856 / *printed*
1485	**SELB** Staatliche Porzellanmanufaktur Berlin after 1763 / *blue*
1486 **1487**	**TIEFENFURTH** (Parowa) P. Donath after 1883 / *printed*
1488	**SAINT AMAND LES EAUX** J. B. Fauquez end of 18th cent. / *blue*
1489	**LONGTON** Salisbury China end of 19th cent. / *printed*
1490	**LONGTON** Salopian Warehouse after 1783 / *printed*
1491	**CAUGHLEY** T. Turner, Salopian China after 1783 / *printed*

1490 SALOPIAN.

1491 SALOPIAN

1492		SARGADELOS L. de la Riva & Co. after 1867 / *printed*
1493		FRAUREUTH Porzellanfabrik after 1866 / *printed*
1494		SAINT CLOUD P. Chicaneau *c.* 1677 / *blue*
1495 **1496**		SCHWARZENBACH O. Schaller & Co. after 1882 / *printed*
1497		ARZBERG C. Schumann after 1881 / *printed*
1498		SCHWARZENHAMMER Schumann & Schreider after 1905 / *printed*
1499		WALLENDORF H. Schaubach after 1926 / *printed*

1500 **1501**		SCHIRNDING Porzellanfabrik after 1907 / *printed*
1502		SCHIRNDING Porzellanfabrik after 1907 / *printed*
1503		SCHLAGGENWALD (Slavkov) J. Lippert & A. Haas 1830—1846 / *printed*
1504		SCHLAGGENWALD (Slavkov) A. Haas 1843—1867 / *printed*
1505	SCHLAGGENWALD	SCHLAGGENWALD (Slavkov) Haas & Czjizek after 1867 / *printed*
1506	*Schlaggenwald* 836	SCHLAGGENWALD (Slavkov) J. Lippert & A. Haas 1830—1846 / *impressed*
1507		SCHLAGGENWALD (Slavkov) Haas & Czjizek 1918—1938 / *printed*
1508 **1509**		SCHLAGGENWALD (Slavkov) Haas & Czjizek 20th cent. / *printed*
1510		SCHLAGGENWALD (Slavkov) Haas & Czjizek 20th cent. / *printed*

1511		SCHLACKENWERTH (Ostrov) Pfeiffer & Löwenstein 20th cent. / *printed*
1512		LANGEWIESEN O. Schlegelmilch after 1892 / *printed*
1513		SCHLOTTENHOF Porzellanfabrik after 1893 / *printed*
1514	*Schoelcher*	PARIS, RUE DU FAUBOURG SAINT DENIS Soelcher 1800—1828 / *red*
1515		SAINT CLOUD H. & G. Trou 1722—1766 / *blue*
1516		ARZBERG C. Schumann after 1881 / *printed*
1517		SCHWARZENHAMMER Schumann & Schreider after 1905 / *printed*
1518		WEISSWASSER A. Schwaig after 1895 / *printed*

1519		KÖPPELSDORF-NORD Schoenau Bros, Swaine & Co. after 1854 / *printed*
1520	SCR	MILAN G. Richard 1874 / *printed*
1521		SELB Gräf & Krippner *c.* 1900 / *printed*
1522		SELB Gräf & Krippner *c.* 1900 / *printed*
1523	H&C? Selb	SELB Heinrich & Co. after 1896 / *printed*
1524		SELB Heinrich & Co. 1904 / *printed*
1525		SELB Heinrich & Co. 1911 / *printed*
1526	H.&.C? BAVARIA	SELB Heinrich & Co. 1905 / *printed*
1527		SELB Heinrich & Co. 1914 / *printed*

1528		SELB P. Müller 1928—1943 / *printed*
1529		SELB L. Hutschenreuther 1858—1920 / *printed*
1530		SELB P. Müller 1912—1924 / *printed*
1531		MITTERTEICH J. Richter & Co. 20th cent. / *printed*
1532		SÈVRES period of the Consulate 1803—1804 / *gold, various colours*
1533		BOCK-WALLENDORF Fasold & Stauch after 1903 / *printed*
1534		FREIWALDAU (Gozdnica) H. Schmidt 20th cent. / *blue*
1535		LONGTON Shelley Potteries 1867 / *printed*
1536 1537		KÖNIGSZELT (Jaworzyna Śląska) Porzellanfabrik after 1860 / *printed*

1538	TIEFENFURTH (Parowa) K. Steinmann G. m. b. H. after 1883 / *printed*
1539	SELB Krautheim & Adelberg G. m. b. H. after 1884 / *printed*
1540	SCHLAGGENWALD (Slavkov) Sommer & Matschak after 1904 / *printed*
1541	LANGEWIESEN O. Schlegelmilch after 1892 / *printed*
1542	SOPHIENTHAL Thomas & Co. after 1928 / *printed*
1543	SORAU (Żary) C. & E. Carstens after 1918 / *printed*
1544	SCHELTEN (Šelty) J. Palme after 1829 / *blue, impressed*
1545	SELB P. Müller after 1890 / *blue*
1546	SPECHTSBRUNN Porzellanfabrik after 1911 / *printed*

1547 1548	*Spode* SPODE	STOKE-ON-TRENT J. Spode *c.* 1790 / *printed*
1549	SPODE Stone China	STOKE-ON-TRENT J. Spode *c.* 1800 / *printed*
1550	Spode *Felspar* *Porcelain*	STOKE-ON-TRENT J. Spode 1800—1833 / *printed*
1551	Spode's Imperial	STOKE-ON-TRENT J. Spode 1800—1833 / *printed*
1552	SPODE SON & COPELAND	STOKE-ON-TRENT J. Spode *c.* 1833 / *printed*
1553	S+S	KRONACH Stockhardt & Schmidt-Eckert after 1912 / *printed*
1554	S.ᵗC.	SAINT CLOUD P. Chicaneau *c.* 1677 / *blue*
1555	STONE coquerol et LEGROS PARIS	PARIS RUE SAINT MERRY Stone, Coquerel & Legros 1807—1849 / *blue*
1556 1557	StPM [eagle crest] St. P. M.	STANOWITZ (Strzegom) C. Walter & Co. after 1873 / *blue*
1558		FENTON Crown Staffordshire China after 1808 / *printed*

1559

STAFFORDSHIRE
FINE BONE CHINA
OF
ARTHUR BOWKER

FENTON
A. Bowker
19th cent. / *printed*

1560

FENTON
Crown Staffordshire China
19th cent. / *printed*

1561

FENTON
Crown Staffordshire China
20th cent. / *printed*

1562

LONGTON
Royal Staffordshire China
after 1843 / *printed*

1563

ROYAL STAFFORD
BONE CHINA
MADE IN ENGLAND

LONGTON
T. Poole & Gladstone
after 1843 / *printed*

1564

ROYAL
STANDARD
BONE CHINA
ENGLAND

LONGTON
Chapmans Ltd
after 1916 / *printed*

1565
1566

LONGTON
C. Amison & Co.
after 1875 / *printed*
c. 1900 / *printed*

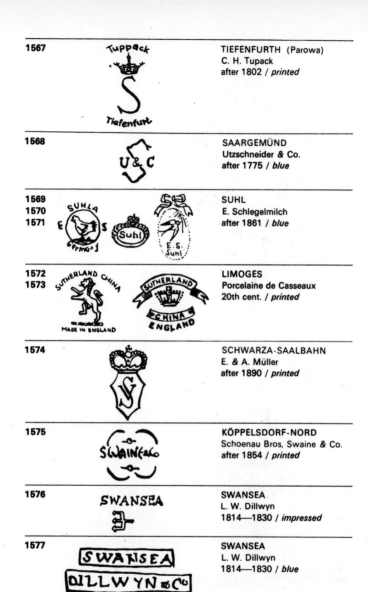

1567

TIEFENFURTH (Parowa)
C. H. Tupack
after 1802 / *printed*

1568

SAARGEMÜND
Utzschneider & Co.
after 1775 / *blue*

1569
1570
1571

SUHL
E. Schlegelmilch
after 1861 / *blue*

1572
1573

LIMOGES
Porcelaine de Casseaux
20th cent. / *printed*

1574

SCHWARZA-SAALBAHN
E. & A. Müller
after 1890 / *printed*

1575

KÖPPELSDORF-NORD
Schoenau Bros, Swaine & Co.
after 1854 / *printed*

1576

SWANSEA
L. W. Dillwyn
1814—1830 / *impressed*

1577

SWANSEA
L. W. Dillwyn
1814—1830 / *blue*

1578

SWANSEA
L. W. Dillwyn
1814—1870 / *blue*

1579	RUDOLSTADT L. Straus & Söhne after 1882 / *printed*
1580 **1581**	SCHWARZENHAMMER Schumann & Schreider after 1905 / *printed*
1582	SCEAUX De Bey, J. Chapelle 1763—1795 / *incised*
1583	LONGTON J. Shaw & Sons 20th cent. / *printed*
1584 **1585** **1586**	TETTAU G. C. Greiner after 1794 / *blue*
1587 	TETTAU G. C. Greiner after 1794 / *blue*
1588	ZWICKAU C. Fischer after 1850 / *blue*
1589 **1590**	TANNAWA (Ždanov) F. J. Mayer 1840—1880 / *impressed*
1591	FRANKENTHAL Carl Theodor von der Pfalz 1762—1797 / *blue*

1592		FRANKENTHAL A. Bergdoll 1762—1775 / *blue*
1593 **1594**		FRANKENTHAL Carl Theodor von der Pfalz 1770—1789 / *blue*
1595		VOLKSTEDT-RUDOLSTADT Porzellanfabrik 20th cent. / *printed*
1596		WALDENBURG (Walbrzych) C. Tielsch after 1895 / *printed*
1597		LUNÉVILLE P. L. Cyfflé; "Terre de Lorraine" end of 18th cent. / *blue*
1598		TETTAU Königliche Porzellanfabrik after 1885 / *printed*
1599		TETTAU Königliche Porzellanfabrik after 1885 / *printed*
1600		TETTAU Gerold & Co. after 1904 / *printed*

1601		**TETTAU** Gerold & Co. after 1904 / *printed*
1602		**TETTAU** Gerold & Co. after 1904 / *printed*
1603		**LIMOGES** C. Tharaud after 1919 / *printed*
1604		**MARKTREDWITZ** F. Thomas 1903—1908 / *printed*
1605		**TILLOWITZ (Tulowice)** R. Schlegelmilch after 1869 / *printed*
1606 **1607** **1608**		**KLÖSTERLE (Klášterec)** Gräfliche Thun'sche Porzellanfabrik 1804—1830 / *blue, gold*
1609		**KLÖSTERLE (Klášterec)** Gräfliche Thun'sche Porzellanfabrik 1830—1893 / *impressed*
1610		**KLÖSTERLE (Klášterec)** Gräfliche Thun'sche Porzellanfabrik after 1893 / *printed*
1611		**ZWICKAU** C. Fischer after 1850 / *blue*

1612 *Tomaszów Mezer*	TOMASZÓW F. Mezer 1806 / *blue*
1613 ☰ ✳ **TOMASZÓW** 1808	TOMASZÓW F. Mezer 1808 / *black*
1614 ☰ ✳ **W TOMASZOWIE** **1808**	TOMASZÓW F. Mezer 1808 / *black*
1615 *w Tornaizo*	TOMASZÓW F. Mezer 1806—1827 / *gold*
1616 *wie* *Tomaszów*	TOMASZÓW F. Mezer 1806—1827 / *gold*
1617	TETTAU Gerold & Co. after 1904 / *printed*
1618 FTP. 1872	POTSCHAPPEL C. Thieme 1872 / *blue*
1619 **T.P.M.**	TIEFENFURTH (Parowa) P. Donath after 1883 / *blue*
1620	LONGTON Trentham Bone China Ltd 20th cent. / *printed*

1621	F:F. *Treviso. 1799*	**TREVISO** Fontebasso Bros 1799 / *blue*
1622 **1623**	G.A.F.F. *Treviso* G.A.F.F. *Treviso.*	**TREVISO** Fontebasso Bros beginning of 19th cent. / *blue*
1624		**TRIPTIS** Porzellanfabrik A. G. after 1891 / *printed*
1625		**COALPORT** W. Taylor *c.* 1820 / *blue*
1626		**POTSCHAPPEL** C. Thieme after 1872 / *blue*
1627		**UPPSALA** Ekeby Aktiebolag from 1918 / *printed*
1628	U D	**DALLWITZ (Dalovice)** F. Urfus 1855—1875 / *impressed*
1629		**UHLSTÄDT** C. Alberti after 1837 / *printed*
1630		**ULM** J. J. Schmidt 1827—1833 / *blue*

1631		**UNTERKÖDITZ** Möller & Dippe after 1846 / *printed*
1632		**SAINT UZE** G. Revol Père & Fils after 1857 / *printed*
1633 **1634**		**VENICE** N. F. Hewelcke 1761—1763 / *incised, red*
1635		**VINOVO** Dr V. A. Gioanetti after 1780 / *blue*
1636		**VINOVO** Dr V. A. Gioanetti after 1780 / *incised*
1637		**VENICE** N. F. Hewelcke 1757—1765 / *red, gold*
1638		**VISTA ALEGRE** J. Ferreira Pinto Basto 1824—1840 / *blue*
1639 **1640**		**VISTA ALEGRE** J. Ferreira Pinto Basto after 1840 / *blue*
1641		**BORDEAUX** M. Vanier 1788—1790 / *blue, red, gold*
1642		**SAINT VALLIER** L. Boissonnet 20th cent. / *printed*

1643	D V G (monogram with cross)	VINOVO Dr V. A. Gioanetti *c.* 1800 / *blue*
1644	*Ven·*	VENICE F. & G. Vezzi 1720—1727 / *blue*
1645	VEN: (with superscript a)	VENICE F. & G. Vezzi 1720—1727 / *blue*
1646	Veni: (with superscript a)	VENICE F. & G. Vezzi 1720—1727 / *red, blue, gold*
1647	Von (with superscript)	VENICE F. & G. Vezzi 1720—1727 / *blue, incised*
1648	Ven: (script)	VENICE F. & G. Vezzi 1720—1727 / *red, blue, green*
1649	*Velvet china* (in circle)	ILMENAU Greiner and successors 20th cent. / *printed*
1650	**Venezia.**	VENICE F. & G. Vezzi 1720—1727 / *blue*
1651 **1652**		LAVENO Società Ceramica Italiana 20th. cent. / *printed*
1653 **1654**		KLOSTER VESSRA Porzellanfabrik 1892 / *printed*

| 1655 |  | VINOVO
Fornari
19th cent. / *blue* |

| 1656
1657 |  | ALT-ROHLAU (Stará Role)
Porzellanfabrik Victoria A. G.
after 1883 / *printed* |

| 1658 | | HOF MOSCHENDORF
O. Reinecke
after 1878 / *printed* |

| 1659 | | LONGTON
Cartwright & Edwards Ltd
after 1851 / *printed* |

| 1660 |  | SHELTON
J. & W. Ridgeway
1850—1858 / *printed* |

| 1661
1662 |  | COBRIDGE
Viking Pottery Co.
1936 / *printed* |

| 1663 | villers Cottereti | CHANTILLY
Villers Cotterets
1770—1785 / *blue* |

| 1664 | | SCHORNDORF
Bauer & Pfeiffer
1904 / *printed* |

1665	*Porcelana de 1850 Vista Alegre em Portugal*	VISTA ALEGRE J. Ferreira Pinto Basto 1850 / *blue*
1666	Vista Alegre Est. 1824	VISTA ALEGRE J. Ferreira Pinto Basto 20th cent. / *printed*
1667 **1668**		VOHENSTRAUSS J. Seltmann after 1901 / *printed*
1669		VOLKSTEDT-RUDOLSTADT K. Ens after 1898 / *printed*
1670	BAVARIA *Johann Seltmann Vohenstrauß*	VOHENSTRAUSS J. Seltmann 20th cent. / *printed*
1671	*VoloKitine miKlachefsKy*	VOLOKITINO A. Miklaszewski 19th cent. / *red*
1672	V.P.	CHODAU (Chodov) Porges von Portheim after 1845 / *impressed*
1673		VOLKSTEDT-RUDOLSTADT R. Eckert & Co. after 1895 / *printed*

1674		**FRANKENTHAL** J. N. van Recum 1797—1799 / *blue*
1675		**BERLIN** W. C. Wegely 1751—1757 / *blue, impressed, incised*
1676		**BERLIN** W. C. Wegely 1751—1757 / *blue, impressed*
1677 **1678**		**WÜRZBURG** C. Geyger 1775—1780 / *impressed*
1679 **1680**		**BORDEAUX** P. & J. Verneuilh 1781—1787 / *blue, gold, red*
1681 **1682** **1683**		**WORCESTER** Dr J. Wall 1751—1783 / *blue*
1684		**LONGTON HALL** W. Littler 1753—1760 / *blue*
1685		**LOWESTOFT** imitations of Worcester porcelain end of 18th cent. / *blue*
1686 **1687**		**WALLENDORF** J. W. Hamann and G. and J. Greiner 1764—1800 / *blue*
1688		**WALLENDORF** J. W. Hamann 1764—1778 / *blue*
1689		**WEISSWASSER** A. Schweig after 1895 / *printed*

1690		VISCHE L. Birago 1766—1768 / *impressed*
1691		HORN H. Wehinger & Co. 1905 / *impressed*
1692		WALLENDORF H. Schaubach after 1926 / *printed*
1693		WISTRITZ (Bystřice) Krantzberger, Mayer & Purkert after 1911 / *printed*
1694		LIPPELSDORF Wagner & Apel after 1877 / *printed*
1695		TURN (Trnovany) E. Wahliss before 1918 / *printed*
1696		MARKTREDWITZ F. Neukirchner after 1916 / *printed*
1697		WALDERSHOF Porzellanfabrik 1907—1924 / *printed*

1698		WALDSASSEN Bareuther after 1866 / *printed*
1699		WEINGARTEN R. Wohlfinger after 1882 / *printed*
1700 **1701**		WEIDEN Bauscher Bros after 1881 / *printed*
1702		BLANKENHAIN C. & A. Carstens after 1790 / *printed*
1703		BLANKENHAIN C. & A. Carstens after 1790 / *printed*
1704		WEISSENSTADT Dürbeck & Rückdäschel after 1920 / *printed*
1705		WEISSWASSER A. Schweig after 1895 / *printed*
1706		OESLAU W. Goebel after 1879 / *printed*
1707		ELGERSBURG E. & F. C. Arnoldi after 1808 / *blue*

1708	WALDERSHOF J. Haviland after 1907 / *printed*
1709	VIENNA, AUGARTEN Porzellanfabrik after 1922 / *blue*
1710	WILHELMSBURG Porzellanfabrik after 1882 / *printed*
1711	WEIDEN C. Seltmann after 1911 / *printed*
1712	VOLOKITINO A. Miklaszewski 19th cent. / *red*
1713	WORCESTER R. Holdship 1751 / *printed*
1714	WEINGARTEN R. Wohlfinger after 1882 / *printed*
1715	SCHORNDORF Porzellanmanufaktur 1904—1939 / *printed*
1716	LUDWIGSBURG Wilhelmus Rex 1816—1824 / *red, gold*
1717 1718	LONGTON HALL W. Littler 1751—1753 / *blue*

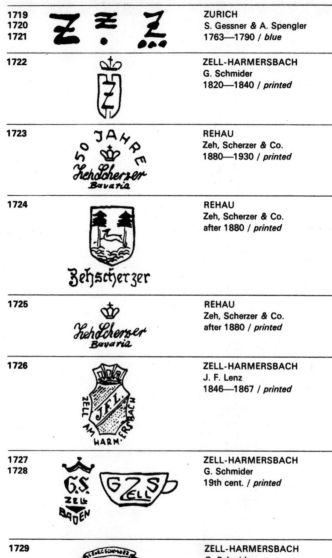

1719 1720 1721	**ZURICH** S. Gessner & A. Spengler 1763—1790 / *blue*
1722	**ZELL-HARMERSBACH** G. Schmider 1820—1840 / *printed*
1723	**REHAU** Zeh, Scherzer & Co. 1880—1930 / *printed*
1724	**REHAU** Zeh, Scherzer & Co. after 1880 / *printed*
1725	**REHAU** Zeh, Scherzer & Co. after 1880 / *printed*
1726	**ZELL-HARMERSBACH** J. F. Lenz 1846—1867 / *printed*
1727 1728	**ZELL-HARMERSBACH** G. Schmider 19th cent. / *printed*
1729	**ZELL-HARMERSBACH** G. Schmider 19th cent. / *printed*

1730	ZELL	ZELL-HARMERSBACH J. F. Lenz 1846—1867 / *printed*
1731		OBERHOHNDORF F. Kaestner after 1883 / printed
1732	J Z & Co	SELB J. Zeidler & Co. after 1866 / *impressed*
1733		SEEDORF Müller & Co. 1907 / *printed*
1734		ALT-ROHLAU (Stará Role) M. Zdekauer 1918—1938 / *printed*
1735		ZWEIBRÜCKEN, GUTENBRUNN Christian IV of Pfalz- Zweibrücken 1767—1775 / *blue*
1736		REHAU Zeh, Scherzer & Co. *c.* 1880 / *printed*
1737		BUDAPEST Zsolnay after 1862 / *printed*

1738		BUDAPEST Zsolnay after 1862 / *printed*
1739		ST PETERSBURG Imperial Factory, Alexander I 1801—1825 / *blue*
1740		ST PETERSBURG Imperial Factory, Alexander II 1855—1881 / *blue*
1741		ST PETERSBURG Imperial Factory, Alexander III 1881—1891 / *blue*
1742		BAKHTEEVO Count Aksenovich 19th cent. / *blue*
1743		VOLOKITINO A. Miklaszewski 1820—1864 / *blue*
1744		MOSCOW, GORBUNOVO A. Popov 1830—1872 / *blue*
1745		MOSCOW, GORBUNOVO A. Popov 1830—1872 / *blue*
1746		ARKHANGELSKOE Prince Yusupov 1827 / *blue*
1747		ARKHANGELSKOE Prince Yusupov 1831 / *blue*

1748		BARANOVKA F. Mezer 1828 / *blue*
1749		BARANOVKA F. Mezer 1826 / *blue*
1750	Б	ST PETERSBURG S. Batenin 1812—1832 / *blue*
1751		BARANOVKA M. Gripari after 1895 / *impressed*
1752	СФ ВБ	FRYAZINO Barmin Bros 1810—1850 / *blue*
1753	*Барминыхъ*	FRYAZINO Barmin Bros 1810—1850 / *printed*
1754		FRYAZINO Barmin Bros 1810—1850 / *printed*
1755	САФРОНОВА С	MOSCOW, NAROTKAYA Safronov 1830—1840 / *blue*
1756	СЗКБ Ф	ST PETERSBURG S. Batenin 1812—1832 / *blue*

1757		**BUDY** M. S. Kuznetsov 1887 / *blue, printed*
1758	Б К.	**NOVOKHARITINO** T. I. Kuznetsov after 1800 / *blue*
1759 **1760**		**ST PETERSBURG** Imperial Factory, Catherine the Great 1762—1796 / *blue*
1761		**ST PETERSBURG** Catherine the Great, court porcelain 1762—1796 / *blue*
1762	ФГ ГУЛИНА	**MOSCOW, RYAZAN** J. Gulyn 1830—1850 / *blue*
1763		**VERBILKI** F. Gardner after 1787 / *blue*
1764 **1765**		**VERBILKI** F. Gardner after 1787 / *blue*
1766		**VERBILKI** F. Gardner after 1787 / *blue, impressed*

1767 1768	Г ℊ	**VERBILKI** F. Gardner after 1787 / *blue, impressed*
1769	б₀	**GORODNITZA** (Horodnica) W. Rulikowski 1856—1880 / *red*
1770	*Городница*	**GORODNITZA** (Horodnica) W. Rulikowski 1856—1880 / *red*
1771	*Городница*	**GORODNITZA** (Horodnica) W. Rulikowski 1856—1880 / *red*
1772		**GORODNITZA** (Horodnica) W. Rulikowski 1856—1880 / *red*
1773	ГИНТЕЬР·Ко	**MOSCOW** T. Gunther & Co. 1818—1876 / *printed*
1774	*Корецъ* *Ф Компаныіна*	**KORZEC** F. Mezer beginning of 19th cent. / *red*
1775	*Корецъ* *Korzec* 90	**KORZEC** F. Mezer beginning of 19th cent. / *red*
1776		**ST PETERSBURG** S. V. Kornilov 1835—1885 / *printed*

1777		
1778		**NOVOKHARITINO** Kuznetsov Bros beginning of 19th cent. / *printed*

| 1779 | | **DULEVO** S. T. Kuznetsov 1832 —2nd half of 19th cent. *printed* |

| 1780 | ЗАВОДА Б КУЗНЕЦОВЫХЪ | **DULEVO** S. T. Kuznetsov after 1889 / *printed* |

1781		
1782		**DULEVO** S. T. Kuznetsov 1832—2nd half of 19th cent. *printed*

| 1783 | | **RIGA** M. S. Kuznetsov 1842 / *printed* |

| 1784 | | **RIGA** M. S. Kuznetsov 2nd half of 19th cent. / *printed* |

| 1785 | С.Т.К РИГА | **RIGA** M. S. Kuznetsov beginning of 20th cent. / *printed* |

1786		
1787		**VOLKHOV** I. E. Kuznetsov 1878 / *printed*

| 1788 | | **BUDY** M. S. Kuznetsov 1882 / *printed* |

1789	ФАБРИКИ М.С.КУЗНЕЦОВА ТВЕР ТУБЕР.	**TVER** M. S. Kuznetsov 1891 / *printed*
1790	С. Г.К. МОРЬЕ П. I.	**MORE** C. Golenichev-Kutuzov 1847—1887 / *blue*
1791		**ST PETERSBURG** Imperial Factory, Nicholas II 1891—1917 / *blue*
1792	АI АI	**MOSCOW, SPASSK** D. Nasonov 1811—1813 / *blue*
1793	БРАТЬЕВЬ НОВЫХЬ	**MOSCOW** Novoi Bros 1820—1840 / *printed*
1794	П.	**ST PETERSBURG** Imperial Factory, Paul I 1796—1801 / *blue*
1795	П П:К:	**ST PETERSBURG** Paul I, court tableware 1796—1801 / *blue*
1796	АП	**MOSCOW, GORBUNOVO** A. Popov after 1872 / *blue*
1797	ПОПОВЫ	**MOSCOW, GORBUNOVO** A. Popov 1800—1872 / *blue*

1798		**VOLOKITINO** A. Miklaszewski 1820—1826 / *blue*
1799	HX	**KUSYAEV** N. Khrapunov 1820—1840 / *blue*
1800		**LENINGRAD** M. V. Lomonosov Factory 1917 *blue*
1801		**LENINGRAD** M. V. Lomonosov Factory 1917 *blue*
1802		**CHINESE PORCELAIN** **A. Reign marks (nien hao)** produced during the Hung Wu period 1368—1399 / *blue*
1803		Hung Wu 1368—1399 / *blue*
1804		produced during the Yung Lo period 1403—1425 / *blue*

1805

Yung Lo
1403—1425 / *blue*

1806

produced during the Yung Lo period
1403—1425 / *printed*

1807

produced during the Hsüan Tê period under the great Ming dynasty
1426—1436 / *blue*

1808

Hsüan Tê
1426—1436 / *blue*

1809

produced during the Hsüan Tê period under the great Ming dynasty
1426—1436 / *printed*

1810

化年製　大明成化

produced during the Ch'êng Hua period under the great Ming dynasty
1465—1488 / *blue*

1811

成化

Ch'êng Hua
1465—1488 / *blue*

1812

年製　成化

produced during the Ch'êng Hua period
1465—1488 / *blue*

1813

成化年製

produced during the Ch'êng Hua period
1465—1488 / *printed*

1814

治年製　大明弘

produced during the Hung Chih period under the great Ming dynasty
1488—1505 / *blue*

1815

弘治

Hung Chih
1488—1505 / *blue*

1816	德年製 大明正	produced during the Chêng Tê period under the great Ming dynasty 1506—1522 / *blue*
1817	正德	Chêng Tê 1506—1522 / *blue*
1818	靖年製 大明嘉	produced during the Chia Ch'ing period under the great Ming dynasty 1522—1567 / *blue*
1819	嘉靖	Chia Ch'ing 1522—1567 / *blue*
1820	慶年製 大明隆	produced during the Lung Ch'ing period under the great Ming dynasty 1567—1573 / *blue*

1821

隆慶

Lung Ch'ing
1567—1573 / *blue*

1822

曆年製　大明萬

produced during the Wan Li period under the great Ming dynasty
1573—1620 / *blue*

1823

萬曆

Wan Li
1573—1620 / *blue*

1824

啟年製　大明天

produced during the T'ien Ch'i period under the great Ming dynasty
1621—1628 / *blue*

1825

年製　崇禎

produced during the Ch'ung Chên period
1628—1643 / *blue*

1826	大清順治年製	produced during the Shun Chih period under the great Ch'ing dynasty 1644—1622 / *blue*
1827	順治	Shun Chih 1644—1662 / *blue*
1828	順治年製	produced during the Shun Chih period under the great Ch'ing dynasty 1644—1662 / *printed*
1829	順治	Shun Chih 1644—1662 / *calligraphic*
1830	大清康熙年製	produced during the K'ang Hsi period under the great Ch'ing dynasty 1662—1723 / *blue*
1831	康熙	K'ang Hsi 1662—1723 / *blue*

1832

produced during the K'ang Hsi period under the great Ch'ing dynasty
1662—1723 / *printed*

1833

K'ang Hsi
1662—1723 / *calligraphic*

1834

produced during the Yung Chêng period under the great Ch'ing dynasty
1723—1736 / *blue*

1835

Yung Chêng
1723—1736 / *blue*

1836

produced during the Yung Chêng period under the great Ch'ing dynasty
1723—1736 / *printed*

1837

Yung Chêng
1723—1736 / *calligraphic*

1838

大清乾隆年製

produced during the Ch'ien Lung period under the great Ch'ing dynasty
1736—1796 / *blue*

1839

乾隆

Ch'ien Lung
1736—1796 / *blue*

1840

produced during the Ch'ien Lung period under the great Ch'ing dynasty
1736—1796 / *printed*

1841

Ch'ien Lung
1736—1796 / *calligraphic*

1842

嘉慶年製

produced during the Chia Ch'ing period
1796—1821 / *blue*

1843

嘉慶

Chia Ch'ing
1796—1821 / *blue*

1844

produced during the Chia Ch'ing period under the great Ch'ing dynasty
1796—1821 / *printed*

1845

Chia Ch'ing
1796—1821 / *calligraphic*

1846

大清
光道
年製
製道

produced during the Tao Kuang period under the great Ch'ing dynasty
1821—1851 / *blue*

1847

Tao Kuang
1821—1851 / blue

1848

produced during the Tao Kuang period under the great Ch'ing dynasty
1821—1851 / *printed*

1849

Tao Kuang
1821—1851 / *calligraphic*

1850	大清咸 豐年製	produced during the Hsien Fêng period under the great Ch'ing dynasty 1851—1862 / *blue*
1851	咸豐	Hsien Fêng 1851—1862 / *blue*
1852		produced during the Hsien Fêng period under the great Ch'ing dynasty 1851—1862 / *printed*
1853		Hsien Fêng 1851—1862 / *calligraphic*
1854	大清同 治年製	produced during the T'ung Chih period under the great Ch'ing dynasty 1862—1875 / *blue*
1855	同治	T'ung Chih 1862—1875

1856

produced during the T'ung Chih period under the great Ch'ing dynasty
1862—1875 / *printed*

1857

T'ung Chih
1862—1875 / *calligraphic*

1858

大清光
緒年製

produced during the Kuang Hsü period under the great Ch'ing dynasty
1875—1908 / *blue*

1859

光
緒

Kuang Hsü
1875—1908 / *blue*

1860

produced during the Kuang Hsü period under the great Ch'ing dynasty
1875—1908 / *printed*

1861

Kuang Hsü
1875—1908 / *calligraphic*

1862	奇石寶 閈之珍	B. Hall Marks Gem among precious wares made of precious stones
1863	奇玉宝 閈之珍	Gem among precious wares made of jade
1864	景濂堂 倣古製	produced according to ancient models in Ching-lien Hall
1865	益右 堂製	produced in the I-yü Hall
1866	仁和館	Jên-ho-kuan after the year 1000 Sung dynasty
1867	樞府	Shu-fu 2nd half of 13th cent. Yüan dynasty

1868	佳玉 器堂	Beautiful vessel from the Jade Hall after 1606 Ming dynasty
1869	堂德 馨 製	produced in the Tê-hsing Hall 1573—1620
1870	福 建 製	produced in Fu-kien Ming dynasty
1871	堂慎 製德	produced in the Ch'ên-tê Hall 1573—1620
1872	芝 蘭 製齋	produced in the Chih-lan Pavilion 17th cent.
1873	玉聚 堂順 製美	produced in the Hall of Beautiful Jade in Chü-shun end of 17th cent.

1874 堂製 林玉	produced in the Lin-yü Hall 1662—1722
1875 堂製 玉海	produced in the Yü-hai Hall beginning of 18th cent.
1876 堂製	produced in the Yu-yü Hall beginning of 18th cent.
1877 堂製 奇玉	produced in the Hall of Precious Jade beginning of 18th cent.
1878 玉海堂製	produced in the Yü-hai Hall 1662—1722
1879 堂製 養和	produced in the Yang-ho Hall 1723—1735

1880		produced in the Tan-ning-chai Pavilion 1736—1795
1881		produced in the Ching-wei Hall 1736—1795
1882		produced in the T'sai-jun Hall 1723—1735
1883		produced in the T'sai-hsiu Hall 1821—1850
1884		produced in the Hall of Big Trees 1821—1850
1885		produced in the ancient manner in the Shên-tê Hall 1820—1850

| 1886 | 蓑溿堂 | The Lü-i Hall
18th—19th cent. |
| 1887 | 大雅齋 | The Ta Ya Ch'ai Pavilion
c. 1900 |

C. Artists' marks

1888	張家造	made by Chang-chia after 1600
1889	壺隱 道人	the Taoist Hu-yin *c.* 1600
1890	王眠	Wang Shou-ming after 1600
1891	建中靖 國年製	produced in the first year of the new establishment of the country 1573

1892	牵金式製 天啟乙丑	made by Chin-shih in the *i chou* year, during the T'ien Ch'i reign 1597
1893	陳文伯塑 萬曆丁酉	modelled by Ch'en Wen in the *ting yu* year, during the Wan Li reign 17th cent.
1894	山人陳德	Ch'en-te the Hermit 17th cent.
1895	尚絲圭	Shang-su 1735—1795
1896	呷岳民	Chung family 13th cent.
1897	岩若 陳囯	Ch'en-kuo 1662—1722

1898

made by Yüan Hsin-hsing
19th cent.

1899

made by Kung Yüan-chi
c. 1700

1900

made by Ch'en T'ien-sui
1662—1722

1901

made by Sheng-kao in the last
day of the fourth month of the
third year of the Chia Ch'ing
reign
1798

1902

Pai-shih
c. 1724

| 1903 | | made by Chiang Ming-hao
1662—1722 |

| 1904 | | Chao-ch'in
beginning of 18th cent. |

| 1905 | | Lai
1662—1722 |

| 1906 |  | made by Liang-chi in the *wu chen* year
1808 |

| 1907 | | made by Chiang Ming-hao
beginning of 18th cent. |

| 1908 |  | made by Li Chên-fa
beginning of 19th cent. |

| 1909 | | made by Wang Tso-t'ing
c. 1800 |

1910		Lai-kuan 17th cent.
1911		Yü-chai c. 1725
1912		Li-chih 18th cent.
1913		made by Wang Ping-jun beginning of 19th cent.

D. Symbolic marks

The eight precious things:

1914		pearl
1915		coin
1916		lozenge (diamond)
1917		mirror

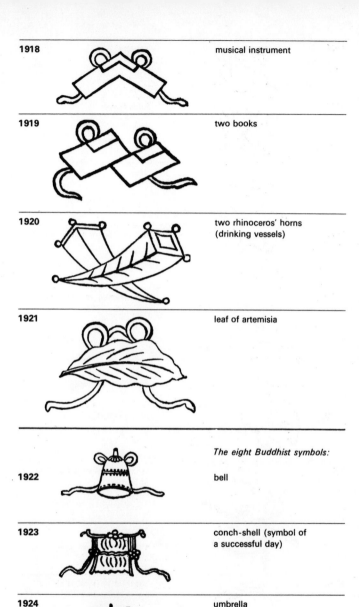

1918   musical instrument

1919   two books

1920   two rhinoceros' horns (drinking vessels)

1921   leaf of artemisia

The eight Buddhist symbols:

1922   bell

1923   conch-shell (symbol of a successful day)

1924   umbrella

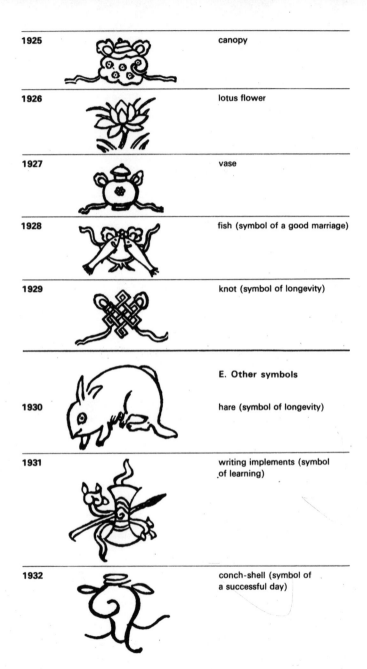

1925 canopy

1926 lotus flower

1927 vase

1928 fish (symbol of a good marriage)

1929 knot (symbol of longevity)

E. Other symbols

1930 hare (symbol of longevity)

1931 writing implements (symbol of learning)

1932 conch-shell (symbol of a successful day)

1933  leaf

1934  leaf (a different form)

1935  mushroom

1936 mushroom (a different form)

1937 peach and bat (symbol of happiness)

1938  musical instrument

1939		eight-petalled flower
1940		five-petalled flower
1941		bud
1942		four-petalled flower

JAPANESE PORCELAIN

| 1943 | | ARITA (Hizen prov.)
Gorodayu Go Shonzui
after 1510 |
| 1944 | | ARITA (Hizen prov.)
Shonzui Gorodayu (imitation)
19th cent. |

1945		ARITA (Hizen prov.) Inscription: wealth, honour and everlasting spring 19th cent.
1946		ARITA (Hizen prov.) Inscription: gem of our precious wares 19th cent.
1947		ARITA (Hizen prov.) Ya (elegance) 19th cent.
1948		ARITA (Hizen prov.) Ho (costliness) 19th cent.
1949		ARITA (Hizen prov.) Fu ku (happiness) 19th cent.
1950		ARITA (Hizen prov.) Kin (gold) 19th cent.
1951		ARITA (Hizen prov.) Ka (prosperity) 19th cent.

1952		ARITA (Hizen prov.) unknown mark 18th cent.
1953		ARITA (Hizen prov.) unknown mark (a Chinese character) 18th century
1954		ARITA (Hizen prov.) Arita (name of city and port) 18th cent.
1955		ARITA (Hizen prov.) Zoshutei sampo (Sampo) 19th cent.
1956		ARITA (Hizen prov.) Hichozan Shimpo 19th cent.
1957		ARITA (Hizen prov.) Fukagawa 19th cent.

1958	三川由 平戸製	**HIRADO** (Hizen prov.) Mikahawacha (factory) 19th cent.
1959	制衣 平戸	**HIRADO** (Hizen prov.) produced in Hirado 19th cent.
1960		**NABESHIMA** (Hizen prov.) imitation of old porcelain from Nabeshima 19th cent.
1961	亀山製	**KAMEYAMA** (Hizen prov.) produced in Kameyama 1st half of 19th cent.
1962	珎玩 道久	**KUTANI** (Kaga prov.) Dosuku (costliness) 18th cent.
1963	九谷	**KUTANI** (Kaga prov.) place mark 19th cent.
1964		**KUTANI** (Kaga prov.) Fu ku (happiness) 19th cent.
1965		**KUTANI** (Kaga prov.) Fu ku (happiness) 19th cent.

1966

KUTANI (Kaga prov.)
Sei (produced in Kutani)
19th cent.

1967

KUTANI (Kaga prov.)
city arms
19th cent.

1968

KUTANI (Kaga prov.)
Fu ku (happiness)
19th cent.

1969

KUTANI (Kaga prov.)
Fu ku (happiness)
19th cent.

1970

九　大
谷　日
造　本

KUTANI (Kaga prov.)
produced in Kutani, in Great
Japan
19th cent.

1971

KUTANI (Kaga prov.)
Tozan (mark representing
the clay used)
19th cent.

1972

KUTANI (Kaga prov.)
Ohi (factory mark)
19th cent.

1973

KUTANI (Kaga prov.)
Shiozo (potter)
19th cent.

1974

KUTANI (Kaga prov.)
Fu ku (happiness)
20th cent.

1975

KUTANI (Kaga prov.)
Tozan (mark representing
the clay used)
19th cent.

1976	大日本九谷製 久錦画圃	KUTANI (Kaga prov.) produced by Yeiraku in Kutani 19th cent.
1977	永樂並 契九谷	KUTANI (Kaga prov.) produced by Kioruku in Great Japan 19th cent.
1978	九谷造 大日本	KUTANI (Kaga prov.) produced in Kutani, in Great Japan 19th cent.
1979	綿野製 景德園	KUTANI (Kaga prov.) Kichii Watano 20th cent.
1980	姫路製	HIMEJI (Harima prov.) produced in Himeji *c.* 1826

1981	東山 播陽	HIMEJI (Harima prov.) produced from Tozan clay 20th cent.
1982	櫻井製	SAKURAI (Setsu prov.) place mark 19th. cent.
1983	吉向	OSAKA (Setsu prov.) Kichiko (potter) 19th cent.
1984	西樂	KOBE (Setsu prov.) place mark 19th cent.
1985	京都	KYOTO (Yamashiro prov.) place mark 19th cent.
1986		KYOTO (Yamashiro prov.) Rokubei (potter) beginning of 19th cent.

| 1987 | | YEIRAKU (Yamashiro prov.)
produced in Yeiraku
beginning of 19th cent. |

| 1988 |  | YEIRAKU (Yamashiro prov.)
place mark
19th cent. |

| 1989 | | YEIRAKU (Yamashiro prov.)
place mark
19th cent. |

| 1990 | | YEIRAKU (Yamashiro prov.)
place mark
19th cent. |

| 1991 | | RANTEI (Yamashiro prov.)
pure jewel from Rantei
19th cent. |

| 1992 | | RANTEI (Yamashiro prov.)
place name
19th cent. |

1993	亀 亭 喜 水 之	KYOTO (Yamashiro prov.) produced by Kisui end of 19th cent.
1994	偕 樂 園 製	KYOTO (Yamashiro prov.) produced by Kisui end of 19th cent.
1995	三 樂 園 製	KYOTO (Yamashiro prov.) produced by Kisui end of 19th cent.
1996	扒 園 造	KYOTO (Yamashiro prov.) produced by Kiyen 19th cent.
1997	大 日 本 香 齋 製	KYOTO (Yamashiro prov.) produced by Kosai
1998	香 齋	KYOTO (Yamashiro prov.) produced by Kosai c. 1850
1999	大 日 本 清 風 造	KYOTO (Yamashiro prov.) produced by Seifu 19th cent.

| 2000 | | KYOTO (Yamashiro prov.) produced by Seifu 19th cent. |

| 2001 | | KYOTO (Yamashiro prov.) Ogari Shuhei (potter) *c.* 1800 |

| 2002 | | KYOTO (Yamashiro prov.) produced by Sahei 19th cent. |

| 2003 | | KYOTO (Yamashiro prov.) carefully produced by Kanzan 19th cent. |

| 2004 |  | KYOTO (Yamashiro prov.) Kenzan (potter) 19th cent. / *brown* |

| 2005 | | KYOTO (Yamashiro prov.) Makuzu Kozan (potter) 2nd half of 19th cent. |

| 2006 | | KYOTO (Yamashiro prov.) produced in Gyokusei 2nd half of 19th cent. |

2007	嘉永元年 南紀男山製	OTOKOYAMA (Kii prov.) produced in Otokoyama 1848
2008		KOTO (Omi prov.) place mark 1830—1860
2009		KOTO (Omi prov.) Meiho (potter) 19th cent.
2010		OVARI (Ovari prov.) place mark 19th cent.
2011		SETO (Ovari prov.) place mark 19th cent.
2012		SETO (Ovari prov.) produced in Seto in Great Japan 19th cent.

2013

加藤勘四郎

SETO (Ovari prov.)
Kato Kanshiro (family of
potters)
19th cent.

2014

SETO (Ovari prov.)
Kawamoto Masakichi
(family of potters)
19th. cent.

2015

SETO (Ovari prov.)
produced by Hansuke in Great
Japan
19th cent.

2016

SETO (Ovari prov.)
tortoise as the mark of local
porcelain
19th —20th cent.

2017

NAGOYA (Ovari prov.)
Kaisha (company producing
enamel porcelain)
20th cent.

2018

NAGOYA (Ovari prov.)
place mark
19th cent.

2019

TOGYOKU (Mino prov.)
produced in Togyoku
19th cent.

2020

TOGYOKU (Mino prov.)
produced by Kato Gosuke
in Mino prov.
19th cent.

2021	日本淡路 賀集三平	SAMPEI (Awaji prov.) Kashu Sampei (place mark) end of 19th cent.
2022		SATSUMA (Satsuma prov.) Hoju (potter) 1780—1800
2023		SATSUMA (Satsuma prov.) Hohei (potter) 1820—1840
2024		SATSUMA (Satsuma prov.) Seikozan (potter) 1830
2025		SATSUMA (Satsuma prov.) place mark 19th cent.
2026		SATSUMA (Satsuma prov.) Hoyu (potter) c. 1840
2027	芳光	SATSUMA (Satsuma prov.) Hoko or Yoshimitzu 1860

2028	サツマ	SATSUMA (Satsuma prov.) mark of the province 19th cent.
2029	薩摩国 慶田製	SATSUMA (Satsuma prov.) Same (shark skin glaze) c. 1888
2030	サツマ 川内	SATSUMA (Satsuma prov.) Bekko (turtle shell glaze) c. 1840
2031	薩制衣	SATSUMA (Satsuma prov.) Satsu Sei (produced in Satsuma) 19th cent.

IMITATIONS OF ORIENTAL PORCELAIN MARKS IN EUROPE

2032	圃	MEISSEN dragon 1723—1733 / *blue*
2033		MEISSEN Yi-hsing on Böttger's stoneware 1710—1720 / *blue*
2034 2035		MEISSEN 1721—1731 / *blue*

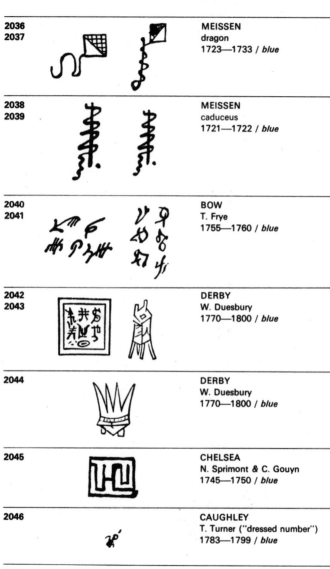

2036 **2037**	**MEISSEN** dragon 1723—1733 / *blue*
2038 **2039**	**MEISSEN** caduceus 1721—1722 / *blue*
2040 **2041**	**BOW** T. Frye 1755—1760 / *blue*
2042 **2043**	**DERBY** W. Duesbury 1770—1800 / *blue*
2044	**DERBY** W. Duesbury 1770—1800 / *blue*
2045	**CHELSEA** N. Sprimont & C. Gouyn 1745—1750 / *blue*
2046	**CAUGHLEY** T. Turner ("dressed number") 1783—1799 / *blue*
2047 **2048** **2049**	**CAUGHLEY** T. Turner 1783—1799 / *blue*

2050 **2051**		**CAUGHLEY** T. Turner 1783—1799 / *blue*
2052		**CAUGHLEY** T. Turner 1783—1799 / *blue, red*
2053		**WORCESTER** 1755—1790 / *blue, red*
2054		**PLYMOUTH** W. Cookworthy 1768—1770 / *blue, red,* *incised in gold*
2055		**STOKE-ON-TRENT** T. Minton from 1821 / *blue*
2056		**RÖRSTRAND** Haancho after 1884 / *printed*
2057		**MITTERTEICH** J. Riber & Co. after 1888 / *printed*
2058		**ANSBACH** Markgräfliche Porzellanmanu- faktur 1757—1790 / *blue*
2059		**VOLKSTEDT-RUDOLSTADT** R. Eckert & Co. after 1895 / *printed*

2060

TURN (Trnovany)
Riessner & Kessel
after 1892 / *printed*

2061

ALT-ROHLAU (Stará Role)
Porzellanfabrik Viktoria A. G.
after 1883 / *printed*

BIBLIOGRAPHY

J. F. Blacker, Chats on Oriental China, *London 1908*

M. Brunet, Les marques de Sèvres, *Paris 1953*

W. Burton, and *R. L. Hobson,* Handbook of Marks on Pottery and Porcelain, *London 1909*

W. Chaffers, Collector's Handbook of Marks and Monograms on Pottery and Porcelain, *3rd edition, London 1952*

L. Chroscicki, Porcelana — znaki wytwórni europejskich, *Warsaw 1974*

J. P. Cushion and *W. B. Honey,* Handbook of Pottery and Porcelain Marks, *London 1956*

L. Danckert, Handbuch des europäischen Porzellans, *Munich 1957*

Geoffrey A. Godden, Encyclopaedia of British Pottery and Porcelain Marks, *London 1964*

J. G. Graesse and *E. Jaennicke,* Vollstänuiges Verzeichnis der auf älterem und neuem Porzellan, Steingut usw. befindlichen Marken. Letzte Neubearbeitung von A. und L. Behse, *22nd edition, Brunswick 1967*

H. Jedding, Europäisches Porzellan, *vol. 1, Munich 1971*

R. M. Kovel and *H. Terry,* Dictionary of Marks. Pottery and Porcelain, *New York 1953*

G. Lukomsky, Russisches Porzellan 1744—1923, *Berlin 1924*

M. Penkala, European Porcelain. A Handbook for the Collector, *London 1947*

E. Poche, Böhmisches Porzellan, *Prague 1956*

R. Rückert, Meissner Porzellan 1710—1810. Katalog der Ausstellung, *Munich 1966*

A. Schönberger, Deutsches Porzellan, *Munich 1949*

M. Swinarski and *L. Chroscicki,* Znaki Porcelany Europejskiej i Polskiej Ceramiki, *Poznań 1949*

C. Jordan Thorn, Handbook of Old Pottery and Porcelain Marks, *New York 1947*

INDEX OF MANUFACTURERS / ARTISTS

241

242

243

244

245

INDEX OF PLACES

250

254